From r

MW00528256

"To keep warm in a cold world you need prayer and meditation. Prayer is to talk to God, and meditation is listening to God."

—Dr. Donald G. King

"Too often do we let the concerns of life, from the mundane routines of the day to grave threats against life itself, distance us from the source of all that is good and wondrous. Engineer Ernst Saint-Louis' boundless enthusiasm for his faith—and his passion for the spiritually troubled—is nothing short of contagious."

—Ed Perratore, Writer/Editor

"*Jesus, the Great Healer* is one of the best reflections about God I have read. Elder Ernst Saint-Louis has created a book that will encourage readers and convert the heart. I was deeply touched when I read the book. Anyone who reads this powerful work of art cannot help but be moved and inspired to become more like Christ in heart, mind and soul. This book is a wonderful work of grace and healing. It will build the faith of our people."

—Dr. Richard A. Marker

"Engineer Ernst Saint-Louis has woven a powerful inspirational work that demonstrates how and why we can keep our faith, whether we're facing deep personal loss or terrifying natural disasters. Using examples from his own experience, he not only puts God's relationship with us into context, but also shows us how we can find the path that brings us closer to Him."

—Michael Gikas, Editor

"*Jesus, the Great Healer* is a step-by-step presentation of Jesus. This is a painstaking work that will lead us well into the praxis of Christianity. The book is filled with practical examples and suggestions that testify to the author's faith."

—Dr. André Célestin

"I find in Engineer Ernst Saint-Louis' book an understanding of his deep sense of faith and his yearning to bring that understanding to others, both within and without that faith. Ernst expounds on each of the major faults of humankind, shows how it manifests in our world and how the Bible sees it, and provides us with hope and a way to climb out of the quagmire into an enlightened life of spiritual joy. This is great reading."

—Engineer Dean Gallea

"In this book, *Jesus, the Great Healer,* the author seeks to amplify the devastating effect sin has had on the earth. The suffering, diseases, crime and terror are evidence that we are living in troublous times. I must agree with the author Ernst Saint-Louis that the only answer and cure to our sick world is Jesus. He can heal our sick world."

—Pastor G. Earl Knight

"Life in this 21st Century is characterized by sophistication, proud prowess, and great progress in many domains. Paradoxically, it is also saturated with fears, tragedies, sorrowful and unexpected events. Only the wise and intelligent can survive in this fast-paced, merciless world and navigates safely to shore. *Ernst Saint-Louis*— in his book *Jesus, the Great Healer*—provides practical pointers to help everyone face the daily challenges of this existence. The book sheds light on how to transform sadness into joy, despair into hope, sickness into health, doubt into confidence, and failures into success. This is a perfect re-source for daily meditation or even small group devotional discussion. I strongly recommend it. It is easy to read. It fills our spiritual voids, and it can make a difference in our life."

—Jean D. François, M.D.

"The book is very fine and expresses Ernst's deep faith and intention to help others. Ernst's meditations are heartfelt and sincere. He whips up an expert mix of Biblical quotes, current events, and original prayers. The result will lift your spirits and help you see the light instead of the darkness."

—Engineer Susan Daino

Jesus, the *Great* *Healer*

Ernst Saint-Louis

Forwarded by Dr. Donald G. King

Also by Ernst Saint-Louis

Jésus, le Grand Guérisseur

Cover Design and Photos: Biblical Perspectives, The Bible for

Students and Atlantic Union College (AUC).

The Millennium Collection of Meditations
Copyright ©2007 by Engineer Ernst Saint-Louis
Mahopac, New York.

ISBN: 978-0-9790381-0-5   0-9790381-0-3

The Millennium Collection of Meditations
P.O. Box 680, Mahopac, NY 10541
E-mail: comeditations@yahoo.com

Printed by Patterson-Printing and

bound in the United States of America.

To the Father, the Son,

and the Holy Spirit,

who give understanding,

wisdom and knowledge!

This book is dedicated to you all...

May *Jesus, the Great Healer* bring

you love, peace, the joy of healing, and

happiness for your entire existence and beyond!

That is my intention for you, and for the world.

In loving memory

of my mother,

Anna Lamartinière Saint-Louis

Jesus, the Great Healer

Thank You Note

I thank very much Mahopac High School Assistant Principal April Tuzman for her enthusiasm and availability. She was my first contact about the translation of the French version.

My thanks go to Dr. Donald G. King, who at great personal sacrifice wrote the foreword for this book, I appreciate his interest, and a level of loyalty that is truly uncommon.

I owe a large personal debt to Donna Tapellini, who at a very early stage took a keen interest in editing the manuscript.

My debts are great to Anne McKay, Jeff Fox, Michael Gikas, Ed Perratore, and Engineer Dean Gallea, for taking their precious time to edit and proofread the manuscript.

How can I forget Dr. Samuele Bacchiocchi, and my friend, Engineer Susan Daino, for their precious help?

I also want to thank Drs. Bordes Henry Saturné, Jean Daniel François, and Robert Jean-Marie Charles, for their support and encouragement.

I would like to thank my family—my wife, Jackie, my daughters, Erline and Jessie, and my son, Eric-Japhet, for their love and patience—even when it meant long hours and other kinds of stress. I especially want to thank my mother, Anna Lamartinière, and my father, John Saint-Louis, for their love and courage, and for teaching me manners and respect for others. I am immensely grateful to God.

Thank you again, Mama! Thank you again, Papa!

Most of all, I want to thank my Jesus, for inspiring and guiding me throughout this monumental task.

Finally, many have contributed from the beginning by their encouragement, and their enthusiasm throughout has helped my efforts to publish this English version.

Meditate, Watch and Pray

Meditate…

about your existence on earth, which is not

by chance. Meditate about what you owe God

and your neighbors.

Watch…

what you say, what you do and what you write, because you will one
day meet your Judge.

A scientist writes: "There is only this life, so live wonderfully and
meaningfully."[1]

—Greg Graffin

No, my friend, this life is not everything.

Death is not, in reality, the end of everything.

Pray…

for the forgiveness of all your sins and your

healing concerns!

May the Lord God Almighty bless you abundantly!

---

[1] OLSON, Steve, Wired magazine, November 2006, p.187.

A world of FEAR:

The clock is ticking, our survival is at stake,

and we are frankly frightened.

Fortunately, some of us are not because

"When you know that a tense drama will turn

out well, even the most anxiety-filled

moments are not as frightening."[2]

The prophet Isaiah describes our God,

the Creator: *"Remember the former*

things of old for I am God, and there is

none else; I am God, and there is none

like me, Declaring the end from

the beginning, and from ancient

times the things that are not yet done,

saying, My counsel shall stand,

and I will do all my pleasure"

(Isaiah 46:9, 10).

$\mathfrak{J}$ sincerely wish with all my heart that

Jesus, the Great Healer will add a new

dimension to your spiritual life, and to

your appreciation of a loving Father,

and lead you to live God's love.

Jesus, the Great Healer is a devotional

guide for everyone to read. Young and

old, believer and non-believer, rich and

poor can learn how to live God's way

and stand by, ready to be with Jesus in

His Kingdom.

I pray that it reaches its objective!

Table of contents

Chapter One

Chapter Two

Chapter Three

Chapter Four

Chapter Five

Chapter Six

Table of contents (continued)

Foreword

This book is special.

That sentence may at first sound like an easily spoken platitude. But a collection of twelve meditations for practical living is no small contribution. In the kind of world in which we live today, where fear and sadness has replaced hope and gladness, we need a collection of meditative gems to periodically remind us that there is a God in control of the Universe. All is not lost. We have a Savior. He is *Jesus, the Great Healer*.

The most casual glance at this book will reveal to even the hurried reader that whatever his or her questions or hurt or need may be one can indeed find hope and strength because of *Jesus, the Great Healer*.

In each of these meditations, you will find candid snapshots of God. He, and only He, can touch those who have experienced suffering, loss, ungratefulness, discouragement, temptation, selfishness and jealousy, hatred, sickness, and sadness. Instead, Jesus brings strength, divine help, healing, joy, complete restoration, deliverance and victory.

For anyone who feels locked behind the iron bars of unfulfilled desires and frustrated dreams, let the words of this collection of meditations inspire you to come forth into the light and gaze earnestly upon Jesus. Look fully into His wonderful face. And the things of this world will grow strangely dim—in the light of His glory and grace. He is, after all, the Great Healer!

—Dr. Donald G. King

$\mathfrak{T}$o the Great Doctor be the glory!

Introduction

In this period of upheaval, confusion, natural disasters, global crisis, war, fear of terror, appalling injustice, and serious diseases that leave even medical doctors helpless and hopeless, one must ask: Is the world hurrying to its end? So many diseases like cancer, heart disease, progeria, Hodgkin's, HIV, cholera, Alzheimer's, Crohn's, Parkinson's, celiac, Lyme, Morgellons, and others cause a great deal of despair. Today there is still no known cure for so many of these diseases. Everywhere on this planet reigns misery, devastation, poverty, incredible violence and vicious crime. A great majority of the world's population lives below the poverty line, and the social disparities are blatant. Unemployment affects poor countries severely, and even the rich countries are not exempt. The heads of states of many countries and their inhabitants are very anxious, agitated and panicked by today's troubling events.

In her address to the French parliament in 2005, Queen Elizabeth II said: "We are living in a dangerous world." Even in developed nations, many people are frustrated, sad, discouraged, discontent and violent. Most recently in France, young French citizens voiced their opinions violently, leaving the leaders panicked and apprehensive. The war against terrorism has claimed so many lives. Many observers fear that something terrible is about to happen in our world. So many calamities defile our world. Indeed, man is facing a challenging and alarming situation. He must choose a path he can depend on: Obey the Lord of lords, serve Him and do good, or obey Satan, serve him and do bad. *"See, I have set before thee this day life and good, and death and evil,"* said the Lord, our Maker (Deuteronomy 30:15). In fact, choices are very important because they have eternal consequences just as sins have terrible consequences.

Contrary to the theory of evolution—no God, no Heaven, no Hell, just Science—the Bible teaches that God has placed us on this earth and our existence is part of His plan. "Science is still only a human endeavor." Besides, God did not create us to live and die in such miserable conditions. According to the Bible, this must not be the end of it. Our world is sick and we need a Great Doctor urgently. Sometimes, it seems that everything is about to collapse. Fortunately, Jesus, the Son of God, said that He is going to prepare a new earth so we can live with Him forever and ever (John 9-11; 14:1-3). He states: "*I and my Father are one*" (John 10:30). Meanwhile, don't look elsewhere for the healing of the world: It is written in Revelation 22:2, there are leaves from the tree that is "*for the healing of the nations.*"

"By distancing themselves from God—humans have also strengthened sin's grip on the natural world. The result is chaos and disorder (Psalms 104:29, 30). The increase of rebellion, apostasy and sin in the last days will result in an increase in natural disasters. But there is another dimension of the interaction between God and natural disasters: Sometimes God uses natural disasters to limit human sin and open new possibilities for His creatures," wrote Angel Manuel Rodriguez, director of the Seventh-day Adventist Biblical Research Institute (Genesis 6:5-8; Amos 4:6-11).

In the Gospel of Luke, the Bible describes the trouble and the confusion we are experiencing today in our world, preceding the return of Jesus, the Master of the heaven and earth: "*Men's hearts failing them for fear, and for looking after those things which are coming on the earth: for the powers of heaven shall be shaken. And when these things begin to come to pass, then look up, and lift up your heads; for your redemption draweth nigh. Heaven and earth shall pass away: but my words shall not pass away,*" said Jesus (Luke 21:26, 28, 33). This self-evident truth was expressed by Dr. Arnold V. Wallenkampf when he writes: "The Bible is very clear about the state of fallen human nature. It's bad, very bad, and if left unchecked it would lead to destruction of the entire human race. All you have to do is look around at the world today. You can see, everywhere the results of what our fallen nature has wrought: addiction, corruption, exploitation, prostitution, kidnapping, terrorism and on and on. It's only because of the grace of God that we haven't destroyed ourselves."

The apostle Paul knew that the last days would be filled with danger and suffering: *"This know also, that in the last days perilous times shall come. For men shall be lovers of their own selves, covetous, boasters, proud, blasphemers, disobedient to parents, unthankful, unholy, Without natural affection, trucebreakers, false accusers, incontinent, fierce, despisers of those that are good, traitors, heady, high minded, lovers of pleasures more than lovers of God; Having a form of godliness, but denying the power thereof: from such turn away"* (2 Timothy 3:1-5). A true description of our world today, isn't it?

Another hot topic is global warming. It is very real. We have done the damage, and we need to talk about repairs. It's our fault. We are responsible for repairing the damage, but somebody has to save this world. The clock keeps ticking. So much time already lost! Very soon, a *Hymnal book* reads, "shall the trumpet give out the welcome sound" for all loyal, faithful, true soldiers, and we will see the King of kings! Don't we need Jesus, such a Savior, who is the Great Healer? He must intervene quickly to contain the anger and wickedness of humanity.

"Humanity is sitting on a ticking time bomb. If many of the world's scientists are right, we have just ten years to avert a major catastrophe that could send our entire planet into a tail-spin of epic destruction involving extreme weather, floods, droughts, epidemics and killer heat waves beyond anything we have ever experienced. If that sounds like a recipe for serious gloom and doom—think again." (—Al Gore, *An Inconvenient Truth.*)

Fearing this alarming signal and convinced of the need for healing, why do you not determine with conviction to obey and serve Jesus, the Great Doctor? Because the Chief Cornerstone is the only sovereign and defender of justice, He will have the last word. You who are sick, who suffer and are traveling a bumpy road, keep faith. "We shall see Him someday." He has the healing medicine. *Jesus, the Great Healer* has already won the battle, and soon we'll be with Him forever. Meet

Jesus of Nazareth today, the Advocate, the Bright Morning Star, the Great Doctor, and you will be healed, fearless, secure and joyful!

Chapter One

Suffering

Suffering is "to feel pain or distress; sustain loss, injury, harm, or punishment. Suffering is the state of physical and emotional pain."[3] Suffering is personal, something others may not easily feel or understand. Natural disasters, disease, terrorist attacks, malnutrition, pollution, ignorance, and intemperance all worsen human suffering. Why is there so much suffering? Throughout the world, particularly in Africa, droughts have killed many people and more than 800 million endure chronic malnutrition. And it's getting worse. Many are in dire need of food and water. Simply put, they are not living a full life. Recently, 400,000 people died in Sudan, with another 2.5 million driven from their homes. Thousands have been raped, tortured, terrorized, kidnapped, beaten, burned, sold, and murdered everywhere. Genocide is ravaging Darfur, Sudan.

Humanity suffers everyday, physically and mentally, from war, crime, urban violence, injustice, hunger, selfishness, unshared resources and further wickedness of man against man. Why does God allow all these things to happen to us? So many suffering people in this world, indeed. Where is God when we suffer? Where was God on the morning of September 11, 2001, when terrorists took down the Twin Towers of the World Trade Center along with the 2,800 souls trapped inside?

---

[3] American Heritage Dictionary, New college edition, Boston, Houghton, 2000.

Where was God in the midst of this inconceivable horror? As a New Yorker on that day, that horrible event dealt me a second blow—it made it impossible for me to take a plane out of New York so that I could bury my recently deceased father in his native land. Where is God? I asked. *Where was God?* Others asked as well, as the death of their loved ones caused them great distress.

September 11 was the big event of the year 2001, but other calamities soon followed. Earthquakes, tornadoes, storms, floods, deadly fires and tsunamis in December 2004, when hundreds of thousands perished, left millions of orphaned children in their wake. Thousands of Haïtians perished in Gonaïves because of the Hurricane Jeanne in September 2004. So many lives changed forever. Many thousands of children lost their lives, and many surviving children in Indonesia and Haïti lost one or both parents. Children—especially those living in poverty—are the most vulnerable victims of a disaster and its aftermath. Recently, a massive earthquake killed more than 70,000 people on the Pakistani side of Kashmir. So many big and sad events, so many victims, and the list keeps growing. Does God abandon us in our difficult times? Regardless, "God will not cast off his people." No, my friend, be assured, the Everlasting Father "will not forsake you." He is here and closer than you think. He will never abandon you, according to His promises. Trust His word. Should we accept God's will in diverse circumstances? "Subjecting to personal suffering, Job then acknowledges that our ability is limited and that the purposes of God are beyond our comprehension" (The Book of Job: Introduction, King James Version). Accept His will with joy because our Advocate knows what He's doing, as He promises in Matthew 28:20, "*I am with you always even to the end of the age.*" And apostle Paul added: "*Who comforteth us in all our tribulation…*" (2 Corinthians 1:4).

"If there was a God, he would have prevented all these…"

Robert Doisneau-Rapho.

September 11, 2001? September 18, 2004? December 26, 2004? God was there. On the issue of suffering, He hasn't left us completely in the dark. We know suffering is the penalty for our sins. Still suffer-

---

September 11, 2001 attacks (Courtesy of APNF/World Trade Center).

ing is not easy to understand. How can one explain such an obscure point? Nevertheless, God is not indifferent to our suffering, to our pain, to our tears and to our miseries. We just fail to grasp the nature and the sovereignty of God. In truth, it is very difficult to comprehend Him. "...*and His ways past finding out!*" (Romans 11:33).

Suffering is a very sensitive subject matter. It can't be answered fully by quoting some Bible passages. However, we can be assured that we will learn a lot more from the Creator when we go to heaven. **Our Maker is alive and He is not impassive**. He is watching over us. "*The fool hath said in his heart: There is no God*" (Psalms 14:1). In reality, my friend, God watches the violence and the wickedness of men. Today again, He suffers and He speaks. That is why the Book of Genesis states: "*And it repented the Lord that He had made man on the earth, and it grieved Him at His heart*" (Genesis 6:5, 6). The Old and New Testaments enlighten us on the suffering of our first parents, Adam and Eve, as well as the suffering of Job, David, Jesus, Paul and others. The Bible also tells us that God knows our suffering, He loves us, and He cares about our deplorable condition. We suffer also when we are trying to help others, but we need to continue to bear one another's burdens regardless because it is God's way, said the apostle Peter: "*For it is better, if the will of God be so, that ye suffer for well doing, than for evildoing*" (1 Peter 3:17). Believe it or not, we are inseparably connected with one another. Some of the following events already mentioned proved this fact. Tragedy in New York, September 2001. Tragedy in Haïti, September 2004. Tragedy in South Asia, December 2004. Tragedy in New York, March 2007: house fire killed nine children and one mother. Tragedy at Virginia Tech University, April 2007: thirty two people shot and killed (the gunman "a student" killed himself). The tragedy of war in Iraq and elsewhere, and so on. Very depressing, indeed? When tragedy strikes, we are all afflicted, aren't we? According to the Bible, God did not want us to suffer and die; that is not in His plans. But the disobedience of our first parents deeply disturbed the order of things, and suffering is the consequence of our sin. At least, part of our suffering in this world is due to our irresponsible behavior and careless actions prohibited by the word of God. Too often we unjustly blame God for our culpability. Because of

The northern city of Gonaïves, Haïti flooded. Over 3,000 people died as a result of flooding and mudslides caused by the tropical storm Jeanne (9/2004 France TV).

sin we are separated from God, as taught by the Bible: *"But your iniquities have separated you and your God, and your sins have hid his face from you, that he will not hear"* (Isaiah 59:2). But God understands and promises His help.

Certainly God is not indifferent to our adversities. God loves us so much that He puts forward a rescue plan for each and every one of us. As a matter of fact, all of man's efforts to escape suffering without His help would be in vain. Because man is so accustomed to doing evil, can he do good? Paul, apostle of Jesus Christ, answers*: "For the good that I would I do not: but the evil which I would not, that I do"* (Romans 7:19). Satan and his followers keep us prisoners of our suffering. But we can be assured that before long his luck will run out, and the Creator will put an end to our suffering. Surely Jesus will come again. Undoubtedly, the entire universe is still under God's control. Our Maker reveals Himself in different ways in the midst of suffering as well as in other difficult situations. Read the Bible and observe all living organisms and their environments, and you will discover that love is Jehovah's main attribute even though His love may be imperceptible and incomprehensible. The Creator of the universe did suffer much, and He is suffering today through our fault. Suffering is part of our everyday life. However, when Jesus comes back, He will eliminate all pain, disease and suffering. According to the Bible, we suffer because of the fall of our first parents. It is inescapable that we suffer and die. In Matthew 13:28, Jesus said, *"An enemy hath done this."* However, in times of trouble and in the burden of suffering, He is not as far away as you might think. In the writings of apostle Peter, God consoles our hearts in our suffering: *"Beloved, think it not strange concerning the fiery trial which is to try you, as though some strange thing happened unto you. If ye be reproached for the name of Christ, happy are ye; for the spirit of glory and of God resteth upon you: on their part he is evil spoken of, but on your part he is glorified"* (1 Peter 4:12, 13). Let's say that I told my two daughters, Erline and Jessie, not to open the fireplace door because they could get burned, and that they did so anyway and were burned. They would then be suffering and in

A massive earthquake in the Indian Ocean triggered sea surges and the deaths of thousands of people (12/2004 Reuters TV).

pain. Inevitably, their mother, Jackie, their brother, Eric, the rest of the family, friends, and I would suffer from their disobedience. I would have compassion for them, would even be willing to suffer in their place. Remember when David heard about the death of Absalon, his son. The king broke into tears. He went up to his room over the gate. He cried as he went, "*O Absalon, my son, my son. If only I could have died for you!*" (2 Samuel 18:33). It is the same for our Father, our Lord, who has compassion for us in our suffering. And He has so much love for us that He gave up His own Son's life to redeem ours. Isn't this magnificent? Our God is marvelous. But the work of Satan, the enemy, is to dishonor Him by creating distrust. Thank God for His compassion, His pity, and His love (Psalms 103:13; John 3:16). In fact, life is empty without the knowledge of God.

Jesus is an actual figure in history who came to seek God's children, to heal the sick, to help those in distress, to feed the poor, to console those who grieved and were oppressed. In his film, *The Passion of the Christ*, Mel Gibson depicts vividly the torture and the inhuman treatment, the humiliation and suffering of Jesus due to our disobedience. However, God always consoles our hearts in our misfortune. He suffered to save us from sin. "*Surely he hath borne our grieves, and carried our sorrows: yet we did esteem him stricken, smitten of God, and afflicted*" (Isaiah 53:4). What suffering for a sweet, a lovely, a humble Redeemer! Jesus' faith in His Father and in the divine justice did transcend, in fact, all His suffering. Voilà! Look at what Christ has done for you! What have you done for Him? Your faith, too, must transcend in Jesus' name, all suffering and adversity. Listen to James Montgomery in *Go to Dark Gethsemane*:

> "In your suffering, see Christ
> at the judgment hall, beaten,
> · bound, reviled, arraigned;
> See Him meekly bearing all;
> Love to man His soul sustained;
> Shun not suffering, shame or loss;
> Learn of Christ to bear the cross."[4]

---

[4] MONTGOMERY, James. (1985). SDA Hymnal Number 157, Hagerstown, Review and Herald Publishing.

The suffering of Jesus Christ (Courtesy of Biblical Perspectives).

Remember, Jesus was killed for doing the work of His Father. We, too, cannot expect to escape the evil of the world and hatred since Jesus, talking with His disciples, said to them: *"If the world hates you, ye know that it hated me before it hated you"* (1 John 15:18). What should we do when confronting evil and suffering? Sin is the source of suffering. Nevertheless, sin was nailed on the cross by the death of Jesus, our Restorer, and the price of our sin was paid at Calvary. *"Take, my brethren, the prophets, who have spoken in the name of the Lord, for an example of suffering, affliction, and of patience"* (James 5:10). Life is difficult, but we have a good and faithful Father who watches over us and provides for our needs with His blessings. So, turn to Jesus for all answers. The Bible is filled with stories of men and women who discover the faithfulness of God in their suffering, sadness and despair. In times of suffering and abandonment, the author of Psalm 22 seeks the Lord, his God, who is always near to those who invoke His name sincerely. And with assured steps the Psalmist says: *"My God, my God, why hast thou forsaken me? Why art thou so far from helping me, and from the words of my roaring?"* And the Lion of the Tribe of Judah provided His assistance to him. He will come to your rescue as well and watch over your life if you seek Him with all your heart! I firmly believe that Jesus can change your situation, and He will support you because He is the supreme God.

Very often our suffering, our anxieties and our pain prevent us from seeing the hand of God, who is ready and willing to assist us. We should be anchoring onto Jesus and to the eternal hope that He puts in our hearts. Unfortunately, we quickly express grievance or resentment about pain and suffering and blame God instead. Feeling anguish, Jesus wanted to step aside from suffering and pain for a little while but finally submitted to His Father's will. It is the same for you who suffer today. However, if you keep faith in Jesus and in His promises, you will be with Him in His glory. After all, we all need to learn to bear the cross of Jesus Christ at least for one bitter hour. My friend! Do not turn away from His grief, because suffering and death in His name surely unlock the gates of heaven and lead us to our Maker for eternal life. According to the Bible, the Lamb of God, in His anguish, looked to His Father for relief.

You, too, in your suffering can look to Jesus, your Savior and your Brother for relief and comfort. Praise His name and give Him glory. Isn't it sweet and reassuring to know that Jesus is near you in times of sorrow and suffering? The prophet Jeremiah says it best in the Book of Lamentations: "*Remembering mine affliction and my misery, the wormwood and the gall...It is of the Lord's mercies that are not consumed, because His compassions fail not. They are new every morning: great is thy faithfulness*" (Lamentations 3:19-23). Yes, you need to anchor onto Jesus, my friend, and remember Jesus is there, He is waiting for you, and He wants to deliver all captives from slavery today. God is waiting for those who are willing to accept His grace. The apostle Paul exhorts the Romans not to give up because suffering is the product of perseverance: "*And not only so, but we glory in tribulations also: knowing that tribulations work patience*" (Romans 5:3). And he added in Romans 8:18, "*For I reckon that the sufferings of this present time are not worthy to be compared with the glory which shall be revealed in us.*" Remember, suffering with Christ is the only road to glory. He is the Truth and the Life.

Are you heavily laden and persecuted? When the pain seems unbearable, turn to Jesus and contemplate the cross. Follow Jesus' path, be obedient and faithful, surrender yourself to the Master, and He will guide your life. The end of the ultimate battle is near. My friend, may God give you the strength to endure the suffering, because the final deliverance is near! Jesus is near you, closer than you think! There will be a new world, a world without suffering and pain, a world without death. It is written, the word of God says so. Would you not want to be part of this new world? (See Revelation 21.) The ultimate battle for domination of the universe is going to end. Once and for all, Jesus will settle the question of suffering and death, and we will have lasting rest and peace forever and ever. You see, God is in control of everything. He gives us hope and assurance in spite of all the suffering because there is deliverance in Jesus. Without Him, nothing is certain today or in the future. Soon, "there will be no dark valley when Jesus comes back and there will be songs of greetings to gather His loved ones home," says a hymnal book.

A prayer:

Dear God, since it is your will for me to suffer, Oh! Father, give me courage, strength and patience so I can see your glory. Help me cling to your word, please. In Jesus' name, I pray. Amen!

With Jesus, suffering turns to joy and gladness. With Jesus, there is deliverance and victory against the enemy, against suffering, against disease, against death and against the forces of evil that enslave you. In any event, be strong in the Lord. Thankfully, His grace is sufficient in this world and in the future. Jesus of Nazareth accompanies you always in pain and suffering!

"Suffering, evil, injustice, death, especially

when it strikes the innocent such as children

who are victims of war and terrorism, of

sickness and hunger, does not all of this put

our faith to the test?" Pope Benedict XVI.

Have faith in *Jesus, the Great Healer*.

Pray, meditate, hope, and wait

patiently for healing!

Suffering turns to joy and gladness

In times of suffering and distress, we all need to stay

close to God because He comforts us so that we can

comfort others: "*For He has not ignored the suffering*

of the needy. He has not turned and walked away.

He has listened to their cries for help" (Psalms 22:24).

Thankfully, Jesus provides strength, patience,

and endurance against suffering.

And the tears of suffering become seeds of joy.

Chapter Two

Loss

Loss: "Detriment, disadvantage, or deprivation from failure to keep, have, or get. It is a condition of being deprived of something or someone."[5] Loss can be individual or collective. It can rob us of our strength and energy and produce disorientation, confusion, and distress. How do we face loss and depression? Throughout our lives, we will experience losses and all forms of disasters, and we must learn to bear them. From time to time, we ask ourselves how to cope with such losses: the sudden death of a parent, a spouse, or a child, a friend, a neighbor, or a colleague. Loss saps our energy and throws us into feelings of disbelief and distress. Sometimes the loss is so profound that it's impossible to contend with the situation and start over again unless a powerful force comes to our rescue. Who can that be? Who is capable enough, powerful enough to reverse such situations and show us the way out? Only the Restorer because He is *"the way, the truth and the life"* (John 14:6). No man can help us the way Jesus can. Besides, He is available all the time and is more than willing to help. Lost or feeling lonely? Frustrated from trying to make it on your own? Jesus is waiting for you. Why are you waiting to go to the Master? Go and pray to Him today because He's capable of resolving any

---

[5] American Heritage Dictionary, New college edition, Boston, Houghton, 2000.

dilemma. Prayer is the only key that I personally know will open the door to God's House, and meditation is God's quickest answer to our concerns. Just as this book went to press, tragedy struck New York again. A deadly fire wiped out the lives of two families from Mali, Africa residing in the Bronx. Ten precious lives perished on one winter night on March 2007— nine children and one mother. How will the other family members cope with such a tragedy? What a sudden loss! They were inconsolable. A great tragedy isn't it? What an unbearable loss! *"So our consolation also aboundeth by Christ"* (2 Corinthians 1:5). Thankfully, as Jesus said: *"I will not leave you comfortless"* (John 14:18). Very often it gets to the point that due to our lack of faith or by ignorance, we go crazy when things go awry and behave as though it's the end of the world. We forget that when everything is lost we still have Jesus. When all the visible and perishable goods are lost, we still have Jesus, the imperishable. Also, we forget that the visible possessions of this world come from the invisible, according to Genesis 2.

My friend, everything on this earth, even the planet itself, is perishable. That is why God's angels are trying daily to detach us from those *perishable* items. Instead, we do every day what Esau did with his birthright when he sold it to his younger brother for a bowl of pottage (Genesis 25). No, my friend! All is not lost because you have Jesus. The invisible things belong to God, and they are spiritual and have real value, while the visible things are material and have no real value because they are perishable. Yes, from the invisible comes the visible: *"And God said, Let there be light: and there was light..."*(Genesis 1). It's a pity that we care more about the material than the spiritual things. By disobeying God, indeed we are voluntarily rejecting the grace of God. Are you sad, loaded with worries, frustrated, or exhausted because you lost everything? Look to Jesus for assistance because He has all the resources to come to your rescue. All you need to do is believe, to trust Him, to be patient and faithful. He will help you to recuperate. Jesus will take the load off your mind. I am sure of it. He did the same for me. He can do it for you, too. Put all your hope in Him. He knows how to connect the dots. Be like David, who implores God's mercy in Psalm 38: *"O Lord, rebuke me not in thy wrath: neither chasten me in thy hot displeasure. For thine arrows stick fast in me, and thy hand presseth me sore. There is no soundness in my flesh because of thine anger; neither is there any rest in my bones because of my sin.*" Even if God doesn't do for you what you expect, trust Him still. God can do wonderful things if you wait for His time, my friend. Just obey Him because He is faithful. Disobeying God brings punishment and sorrow but obeying Him brings joy and happiness today and tomorrow!

If you have lost everything, God can give you the opportunity to make a fresh start. He loves you, and He wants to see you happy. He is willing and waiting for your request. But if God doesn't satisfy your expectations, you are going to have to wait. He is the owner of the universe. The trouble is that what may seem like the right time for you may not be the ideal moment for God. You need to learn to cultivate patience. Jesus once said: "*Woman, what have I to do with thee? Mine hour is not yet come*" (John 2). Yes, God gives opportunities to start over. Very often, His time is not our time. Patiently, just wait on the Lord's time because His time is invariably the ideal time. Therefore, our Advocate is always on time no matter how long we have to wait. In times of sorrow, persecution and tribulation, pray and wait on the Man of sorrows for comfort. In any event, He hears the prayer of the troubled heart for deliverance because He is sympathetic and compassionnate.

As Jesus said: "*...I will come to you*" (John 14:18). In a letter to the Philippians, the apostle Paul spoke about loss: "*But what things were gain to me, those I counted loss for Christ. Yea doubtless, and I count all things but loss for the excellency of the knowledge of Christ Jesus my Lord: for whom I have suffered the loss of all things, and do count them but dung, that I may win Christ*" (Philippians 3:7-8). Your loved one may be gone; storm or fire may have destroyed everything. You may have no more friends, and you may be lonely, without assistance. Let me tell you that you have a true Friend in Jesus. Personally, I believe that with Jesus not only you do have a Friend, you have a faithful Companion, too. In truth, how do you continue your daily activities and learn to accept losses without Jesus? In distress God promises His help, and He's ready to bless you. He's ready to give you peace and joy. His grace is sufficient. Loss always brings pain, misery and tears, but the word of God exhorts us to meditate on Job's attitude when he had lost everything. Despite such big losses, he remained confident in the Lord's kindness. After all, Job understood that God is the owner of everything. That is why he said, courageously: *"The Lord gave, and the Lord hath taken away; blessed be the name of the Lord"* (Job 1:21). Very inspiring words—and edifying, too! Job understood God's message and humbled himself. God healed Job and gave him peace, joy, wealth and a happy family. He can do the same for you, too, because He is the same God yesterday, today, and tomorrow. If your business is not working well and you are anxious, your perspective on life is more and more gloomy. Have you lost everything? If so, just remember, you still have Jesus, the Great Provider.

In the year 1990, as an electronics engineer with a computer-maintenance background, I decided to open my own business. In the beginning, the Lord did bless me and continued to do so as the years passed by. Later on, though, things started to fall back due to fierce competition in the computer industry and lack of funds. Part of this is because I lost money trying to open another branch of business overseas. I was struggling to resolve my loss, but my financial situation got weaker. After nine years in business, I decided to close shop. I even started to doubt God's promises. More or less, however, I kept faith; I never stopped praying, meditating and trying to understand what had happened and how to cope with the debt I inherited from the business. There we go, we thought, we lost everything, but it is not the end. Jesus opened doors, and I had the blessed privilege to choose which one to enter. Yes, new doors opened. Truly, Jesus is good all the time. If you have Jesus He will take care of you. Isn't that extraordinary? What a loving and passionate Provider! He did it for me so He can do it for you, too! I felt obligated to share my experience with others because I am sure Jesus will strengthen your faith and help you as He did for me and for others as well. I have learned with God that everything is possible since I have been there. *"Do I lack strength to rescue you?"* In fact, *"Is any thing too hard for the Lord?"* asks God in Isaiah 50:2 and in Genesis 18:14. My friend, is all lost? He rescued me. He can rescue you, too! Are you on the verge of losing your property, your car, your home or your business? Heavy burdens? Feeling despised and rejected? I can't afford not to tell you to trust Jesus. You see, trust is essential.

You need to have faith, discipline and perseverance. Tired of running fast? Feeling lonesome? Yes, it's time for a change. Jesus says: *"Take my yoke upon you, and learn of me; for I am meek and lowly in heart: and ye shall find rest unto your souls. For my yoke is easy, and my burden is light"* (Matthew 11:29-30).You need to trust Him because without trust you will not get far. My friend, commit your soul to Jesus. Trust Him enough to follow Him through adversity, privation and suffering. I trust you will do just that because things work out only if one trusts the Master. Thankfully, your Provider is just around the corner, and He wants to accompany you in your loss. Don't lose faith. Stay afloat, because help is on the way. Our Jesus is marvelous! Our awesome God cares! Fortunately, if we choose to live by and obey His commandments, we will receive many blessings. Jesus is your Friend. He is with you in times of adversity and loss if you trust Him. Of course, you will encounter many adversities in life. Choose Jesus today because He is closer than you think. Believe it or not, He is the answer to all our needs, not man. With Him as your Shepherd, there is hope, safe refuge, and strength in times of trials, persecutions, and distress.

> "Father, Lead me Day by Day,
> Ever in Thine own sweet way;
> Show me what I ought to do.
> When in danger, make me brave;
> Make me know that Thou canst save;
> Keep me safe by Thy dear side;
> Let me in Thy love abide.
> Father, Lead me Day by Day."[6]

All is lost. With the Redeemer, it is well!

Even though it is sometimes hard to feel the presence of Jesus, keep your eyes focused on Him because He is in control. His grace is

---

[6] NEWTON, John. (1985). SDA Hymnal Number 482, Hagerstown, Review and Herald Publishing.

sufficient in this world and in the world to come. Jesus of Nazareth gives strength to start anew because He loves and cares for us!

Chapter Three

Ungratefulness

What is ingratitude? "The state of being ungrateful; unthankful[7]" Ingratitude is the result when anyone denies and fails to recognize the need to be grateful and to express gratefulness towards a benefactor. The Bible mentions multiple cases of the ingratitude of man towards the Maker and man towards man. From whom do we receive blessings? What is the role of those who receive them? Our society is very cold, hopeless, frustrated and stressful. So many things are out there for managing stress, but none of them can eliminate stress. Even though some stress is needed to make life challenging, it remains a fact that gratefulness, an "attitude of gratitude," and thanksgiving can help us handle stress. Everything we have comes from God. All are His belongings. Shouldn't we be grateful towards Him? Isn't it from Him that we receive all kindness? So doesn't He deserve our gratitude? God is our Benefactor. Therefore, we must be grateful to Him and to those who helps us. God's throne is in heaven. He is the Creator of heaven and earth. Creation of the Universe was His labor. Doesn't He deserve our worship? Aristotle, the philosopher, once said: "Gratefulness is

---

[7] Unabridged Dictionary, Random House, New York, 2006.

necessary to maintain friendship." The Bible teaches us that a woman called Mary demonstrated her gratitude towards Jesus by washing her Savior's feet with an expensive perfume. It was a gesture of friendship welcomed by Jesus, in spite of the negative interventions of a few selfish, avaricious and hypocritical disciples. Jesus responded: "*Why did you make that woman unhappy? She did something good towards me.*" And when Judas made his remark about giving the proceeds of the sale of this perfume to the poor, Jesus said simply: "*For the poor always ye have with you; but me ye have not always*" (John 12).

Should we continue to be kind to the ungrateful? In the parable of the lepers, ten were healed but only one came back to Jesus to give Him thanks: "*Where are the other nine, were there not ten cleansed? Jesus asked. There are not found that returned to give glory to God, save this stranger. And Jesus said unto him, Arise, go thy way: thy faith hath made thee whole*" (Luke 17:12). For the grateful Samaritan leper, being thankful was an obligatory debt. And it should be no less for you and I. Jesus knew long before that nine of the ten were not going to give glory to the Creator. However, they all received His blessings. Indeed, we all need to practice the gospel of relationship! Jesus is good to the grateful and ungrateful alike. So we must also continue to do good to both to the end. And Jesus stated clearly: "*Be ye therefore merciful, as your Father also is merciful*" (Luke 6:36). Apostle Luke, the "beloved physician" speaks of God as the Creator and the Father of all and everyone: "*And Jesus lifted up His eyes on His disciples, and said: ...the highest is kind unto the unthankful and to the evil.*" (Luke 6:35; 17) What Luke is telling us here?
-We must at all times do as Jesus did!

King David expressed his gratefulness towards Mephi-Bosheth, because Mephi-Bosheth's father came to his rescue when Saul, Jonathan's father, wanted to kill David (2 Samuel 9). The psalmist David recognized the need for gratitude and invited us in Psalm 103 to bless God constantly: "*Bless the Lord, O my soul: and all that is within me bless his holy name. Bless the Lord, O my soul, and forget not all his benefits: Bless the Lord, all his works in all places of his dominion: bless the Lord, O my soul.*" Ingratitude is a negative and self-destructive attitude. We all have to confess our sin of ingratitude towards God and ask for forgiveness. Be always grateful to the Maker and the Provider. The psalmist David was a man of God, a grateful servant of the Lord. That explains why he is a man after God's own heart (Acts of the Apostles13:22). It is an undeniable fact that only God's grace makes us grateful. The Bible also mentions God's advice to the Israelites about ingratitude: "*And houses full of all good things, which thou filledst not, and wells digged, which thou diggedst not, vineyards and olive trees, which thou plantedst not; when thou shalt have eaten and be full; Then beware lest thou forget the Lord, which brought thee forth out of the land of Egypt, from the house of bondage*" (Deuteronomy 6:11, 12).

Never be like the ungrateful who turned away from the Provider after receiving His blessings. Always give Him the first place in your heart, and you will have Jesus' joy and peace. In reality, God's truly amazing grace heals and sustains us every day. That is why we should celebrate Him and bless Him for His marvelous grace and His indescribable love. Give thanks for everything because the Maker, *Jesus, the Great Healer* deserves our praise for His kindness and His compassion. Be thankful and praise the Provider in all circumstances. And Fanny Crosby, in *To God be the Glory*, goes further:

"To God be the glory,
Great things He hath done;
Great things He hath taught us,
And great our rejoicing through Jesus, the Son;
Praise the Lord, Praise Him!"[8]

You see, our Creator deserves our gratefulness. The feelings of gratitude that you and I enjoy come from the grace of Jesus! Humbly, Jaïrus asked Jesus to heal his sick daughter. He went to his home and ordered the young woman to get up. And she became alive again. (See Luke 8.) Isn't it superb? To conquer ungratefulness, you need to develop an attitude of thanksgiving.

---

[8] CROSBY, Fanny. (1985). *SDA Hymnal* Number 341, Hagerstown, Review and Herald Publishing.

We need to live a grateful life. The Bible reveals that Jaïrus' family was very grateful towards Jesus for resurrecting their daughter. And the apostle Paul wrote: "*and be ye thankful*" (Colossians 3:15). I too, and my family experienced God's mercy and His goodness, and we are grateful to Jesus because of His love towards us. He has done great things for us, and we should praise His name forever! Don't be mistaken, He can do great things for you, too, and even more if you surrender your life to Him today! May Jesus help you to have an "attitude of gratitude"! What am I thankful for? So many things to be thankful for: give thanks to the Almighty for all His daily blessings: water, food, health, oxygen, shelter, security, etc. Stop for a moment and add to this list for yourself. Count your blessings, and name them one by one. Could you list them? Truthfully they are countless.

1)
2)
3)
4)
5)
6)
7)
8)
9)
10)
11)
12)

Use an additional sheet if necessary to count your blessings. You should sing His praises because He is faithful and His love endures forever. Unfortunately, the world is sick, hostile and ungrateful. Remember to be thankful in good as well as bad times. Our Jesus is a superb Deliverer! The ancient philosopher Cicero said: "Gratitude is not only the greatest of virtues, but the parent of all the others." May Jesus help you to live an abundant and a grateful life! In his writings, it is interesting to note that Paul always begins with "salutation and thanksgiving": "*In every thing give thanks: for this is the will of God in Christ Jesus concerning you*" (1

Thessalonians 5:18). Our Creator deserves our gratefulness for all the blessings. Give thanks to the Lord of good and put behind the guilt of ingratitude! We need to develop an attitude of thanksgiving because Jesus gave us so much: life, health, air, the sun, water, food, clothing, shelter, family, children, and friends. Let us all have an "attitude of gratitude"!

A prayer:

My God and my Father, I would like to be grateful for your favors, because the fact is that only you can put this feeling of gratefulness and humility in my heart. Please have mercy upon me and give me the feeling of gratitude. In Jesus' name, I pray!

Frankly, it is the feeling of gratefulness that Jesus puts in our hearts, which stirs us to give glory and praise to God for His kindness, because His grace is sufficient here and in the world to come! Only Jesus of Nazareth can give this feeling of gratefulness and humility!

Chapter Four

Discouragement

Discouragement is "the condition of being discouraged, loss of physical and moral strength accompanied by renunciation. It may be caused by frustration, anxiety, fear, challenges and other reasons."[9] It's like an epidemic, an infectious disease that seems insurmountable, and a "pest" to avoid at all costs. It is also a nuisance that must be rooted out vigorously with an efficient antidote. Discouragement is a bad counselor. Guilt, loss, rejection, fear, mistakes, privations, deceptions, obstacles, persecutions and other complicated situations bring feelings of harassment and dejection daily. Discouragement is Satan's powerful weapon against the human race. Perhaps you're feeling a lack of satisfaction, of being overwhelmed and depressed, or lonely and afraid. You may feel as if you've done something wrong and are remorseful. Are doubt, despair, and discouragement taking control and leaving you hopeless? You are not alone. Just let Jesus fill you with hope in times of trial and suffering. There has to be a better way. In the midst of discouragement we all react the same way—with fear and dread. All of us, that is, except Jesus. Maybe while you're reading this meditation

---

[9] Unabridged Dictionary, Random House, New York, 2006.

you are wrestling with discouragement due to lack of understanding of your parents, your spouse, your son, your daughter, your colleague, your friend, or your neighbor. Maybe you have a gigantic task to accomplish, and you don't know where to begin, or nothing works for you and you are in despair. You are very stressed, depressed, alcoholic, doing drugs, or on medication for depression. Right now, you may be fighting HIV, cancer or other diseases, and you are discouraged. For that, the apostle Paul offers comfort and encouragement to Jews, Greeks, as well as Gentiles in Thessalonians 2:11; 3:3: "*As ye know we exhorted and comforted...That no man should be moved or discouraged by these afflictions: for yourselves know that we are appointed thereunto.*"

Remember, the Bible clearly says: even God's servants knew discouragement. Noah was discouraged by the time it took to build the ark, and he was certainly mocked by his friends, his neighbors and strangers for a long time. All this was more than enough to discourage him in spite of his faith, but he found strength in His Lord to pursue God's command. What is left to do, except go to Jesus of Nazareth, the Deliverer. The living God who promises to help will deliver you! Put all your trust in Jesus and do not let yourself crumble. Be faithful and believe in the Maker who gives strength to those in distress for the simple reason that He is God and His promises are truthful: "*God is not a man, that he should lie; neither the son of man, that he should repent: hath he said, and shall he not do it? Or hath he spoken, and shall he not make it good?*" (Genesis 6; Numbers 23:19). Speak to Jesus about all your worries. Lay on His shoulders all your burdens, and He will help you. Go, hurry! And tell Him: "Have mercy on me, Lord, for I am discouraged," and you will have peace, and strength. His faithful love will calm your fear. In fact, His grace is sufficient to do all these things and more. Our Lord and Savior also knew discouragement, but He was victorious. For that reason, you are invited to look up to Him if you want to defeat disappointment.

Yes, the Bible is filled with stories of God's wonderful people who knew discouragement and despair—Abraham, Moses, David, Elijah, Ann, Jeremiah and others. But they knew how to put their trust in the Lord. Thankfully, Jesus has the cure to root out the virus of discouragement. He promises to change our complicated situations. And the Book of Hebrews says: "*For consider him that endured such contradiction of sinners against himself, lest ye be wearied and faint in your minds*" (Hebrews 12:3). The Bible says: Jesus will restore all things. So if discouragement often causes affliction, it helps to know that Jesus always comforts. You may be anxious, disappointed, in dismay and wondering how you are going to make it through the day or through the night. You may be confused, depressed and ready to give in to discouragement. No, stop right there!

In his letter to the Christians in Galatia, the apostle Paul writes: "*Do not get discouraged and give up, for we will reap a harvest of blessing at the appropriate time*" (Galatians 6:9). The prophet Elijah, king Jehosaphat, and Moses were discouraged. Read carefully the stories of the prophet Elijah and king Jehosaphat: 1 Kings 19 relates that the prophet Elijah was charged by God to bring back His lost people, the Israelites—an impossible mission for the prophet Elijah, who escaped in the desert because Jezebel, wife of Jeroboam, king of Judah was after him. Afflicted and crumpled, the prophet said, "*It is enough; now, O Lord, take away my life.*" As in 2 Chronicles 20:2, for the children of Ammon and Moab (a great multitude) stood up against Judah, king Jehosaphat was overwhelmed and discouraged. The prophet Ahaziah said: "*Hearken ye, all Judah, and ye inhabitants of Jerusalem, and thou king Jehosaphat, Thus saith the Lord unto you, Be not afraid nor dismayed by reason of this great multitude; for the battle is not yours, but God's*" (2 Chronicles 20).

The mighty God gave the prophet Elijah the power of victory over the idols of Jezebel. The same scenario happened for king Jehosaphat. The prophet Ahaziah and the king called upon the Almighty for help. He showed up, and all their enemies were defeated. The king and his men returned home happy because the Lord gave them victory over discouragement. Today, the King of Jews can do the same for you, too, and much more. He still has the power. Moses also was displeased with the Israelites and asked God to take away his life. My friend, you are called to chase away the darkness of discouragement and fear with prayer. It helps to know that Jesus soothes pain, gives strength and peace. His presence puts joy in your heart today and in the days to come, since His grace is sufficient daily. Thankfully, God promises relief in times of trials and persecutions as well as in times of discouragement and afflictions. Many Biblical heroes struggled with doubt, and David was one of them: "*In the multitude of my thoughts within me thy comforts delight my soul*"(Psalms 94:19). Discouragement is the enemy seed. What can you do to manage it? It comes from the devil. Nonetheless, if you are discouraged, there is a way out for those who trust and put all their confidence in Jesus. The only solution is to root it out with prayer. Prayer must be the first step for anyone who feels discouraged. Ann, the Lord's servant, was infertile, sad and discouraged. She went in to the temple with tears to meet her God: "*And she was in bitterness of soul, and prayed unto the Lord, and wept sore*" (1 Samuel 1:10).

The Everlasting Father gave her victory over discouragement. Believe it or not, discouragement can leave you in a state of doubt and uncertainty about God's love and draw you away from His divine presence. Stop worrying today and do as Ann did, and you will see His power. If you are struggling with doubt and hardships and you are feeling hopeless, do not panic. I know a Great Doctor. His name is Doctor Jesus. You need to cling to Him. In *Day of Judgment, Day of Wonders!*, John Newton gives praise and glory to God, who gives us strength and puts in our hearts the blessed and beautiful hope that brings comfort when circumstances in life incite discouragement:

> "Day of judgment, day of wonders!
> Hark the trumpet's awful sound,
> Louder than a thousand thunders,
> Shakes the vast creation round!
> See the Lord in glory nearing,
> Clothed in majesty divine.
> You who Long for His appearing,
> Then shall say, 'his God is mine!'
> Gracious Savior, Own me in that day as Thine."[10]

---

[10] NEWTON, John. (1985). SDA Hymnal Number 418, Hagerstown, Review and Herald Publishing.

Finally, God has brought you this far. I am convinced He will not abandon you. That is why we must go to Him for relief. The psalmist encourages us to make a vow to God because He is capable of doing everything possible to lift our spirits and give us the strength we need. The fact of the matter is, no one can resist God, and how dare you! Worries, obstacles, and difficulties harass and invade your souls and leave you helpless, discouraged and despairing. I invite you to focus on the power of Jesus. Go now to Jesus, and He will give you strength and vigor. Yes, He has a powerful weapon against the virus of discouragement. Indeed, His weapon can uproot the virus efficiently. It is a powerful antidote that one can find only in Jesus' supermarket, where everything can be found and you don't need cash or a credit card. There you will find a real and true friend in Jesus, the Almighty God. Stand firm against the disease of discouragement, and do not let it draw you away from *Jesus, the Great Healer*. Nevertheless, if you are discouraged, depressed, and hopeless, His arms are always open, and His ears are as well. Without a doubt He hears your voice as it cries for help in the desert of discouragement because His grace is sufficient in this world and in the world to come! The tribulation has finally passed. Glory to the highest, our Almighty God! Feeling weak and daunted? Don't know where to turn for strength? Turn to Jesus and make Him your supreme Counselor. Humbly, I advise you not to try to remove God from your equation because it is an impossible task. The word of God superbly "conveys the thought of a helper always at hand with counsel, strength, exhortation, or whatever help is needed…" Arnold V. Wallenkampf.

A prayer:

Dear Father in heaven, help me deal with all the unforeseen circumstances of life. Put your strength in my weakness. Help me, please in times of affliction and disappointment! I pray in Jesus' name. Amen!

Affectionately, Paul exhorts the Thessalonians as well as you and I to pray more: *"Rejoice always. Pray without ceasing."* (1 Thessalonians 5: 16, 17). Truthfully, there is power in prayer! No, my friend, do not get discouraged in times of afflictions, and trials because your Maker will meet your needs and your concerns at just the right time.

I conclude this meditation by inviting you to make the Man of Galilee your fellow traveler, your companion, and may He be your passport! By the way, after all He has done for you, don't you want to enjoy His fellowship forever? Jesus of Nazareth can give you strength and vigor in the midst of discouragement!

Strength

Strength is "the quality or state of being physically or mentally strong."[11] Strength is physical and spiritual. Power, wealth, beauty belong to God, Creator of the Universe. There is no situation that God cannot control. Strength lies in Christ. The Bible says, *"The Lord is slow to anger, and great in power"* (Nahum 1:3). Jacob has learned that man's power and desire are in opposition to God. Often defeated and persecuted by his peers, Jacob gained a firm and rare discipline that led him to victory with his God. Jesus is the sole owner of the real force. King David recognized that the force belongs to God and only to God. That is why king David blessed Him in the presence of His congregation: *"Wherefore David blessed Lord before all the congregation: and David said, Blessed be thou, the Lord God of Israel our father, for ever and ever. O Both riches and honor come of thee, and thou reignest over all; and in thine hand is power and might; and in thine hand it is to make great, and to give strength unto all"* (1 Chronicles 29:10-12). If your force fails you, turn yourself to Jesus who has the power to refresh you physically and spiritually. Yes, God rules the universe by His power. Who can oppose Him? The power is only in Jesus! The power of Jesus is in God, the Father. He offers and gives it at His will. Let me reassure you that if you put your confidence

---

[11] Roget's New Millennium, Lexico Publishing Group, New York, 2006.

in Jesus, there is no danger for those who trust the Lord. He is very powerful against the forces of evil. Won't you trust Him? With Jesus we are powerful, we are the winners, and we have security. Only Jesus can defeat the implacable enemy, Satan, since the force is in Christ. Jesus found strength and security in His Father while He was on earth defending our cause. We, too, can find security, peace and strength in God regardless of terrorist threats and any other difficult circumstances. I think, after all, my friend, the real fear is that you do not have Jesus in your heart. Troubled soul? Drinking too much? Heart problems? Undergoing extreme stress? Handicapped? Turn to Jesus for strength. In diverse circumstances, David finds refuge and strength in his Lord even in the shadow of death: *"The Lord is my shepherd; I shall not want"* (Psalms 23:1). How wonderful it is to know that whatever the circumstances we face in this life, we have Jesus of Nazareth. Besides, through His sacrifice, He has made eternal life ours. The choice is yours!

The children of Israel did evil again in the sight of the Lord; and He delivered them into the hands of the Philistines for forty years. *"And the angel of the Lord appeared unto the woman, and said unto her, Behold now, thou art barren, and bearest not: but thou shalt conceive, and bear a son. Now therefore beware, I pray thee, and drink not wine nor strong drink, and eat not any unclean thing"* (Judges 13:3, 4). The newborn's given name was Samson. He had the lion's strength. But where did it come from? In Judges 16, it is written: *"So his strength was not known."* He was one of the faithful servants of God conceived to deliver Israel from the Philistines. He was a symbol of Jesus, the Lord of deliverance. However, his alliance with the Philistines cost him dearly. And the Spirit of the Lord left him. As it says in the Book of Judges, chapter 16:21: *"But the Philistines took him, and put out his eyes, and brought him down to Gaza, and bound him with fetters of brass; and he did grind in the prison house."* Samson, the strongest man looked very weak now. But what could he do? *"Then the lords of the Philistines gathered them together for to offer a great sacrifice unto Dagon. And they praised him. They made Samson stand between the two pillars that held up the roof and the Philistines made fun of him. Then Samson prayed to the Lord: O Lord God, remember me, I pray thee, and strengthen me, I pray thee, only this once, O God, that I*

Samson pulls down a Temple (Courtesy of The Bible for Students).

may be at once avenged of the Philistines for my two eyes..." (Judges16). Samson pushed an entire building down. The Lord gave him back his strength to avenge the loss of at least one of his eyes. But Samson's bad choice hurt him as well as the Philistines. In the first place, the story teaches us that strength comes from God. In the second place, terrible consequences result from bad choices. Trust God and wait for His intervention. If worries and disappointments make you feel weak, Jesus tells you today: be strong in the Lord because He will put His force in your weakness. Yes, there is power in the blood of Jesus. The same God that fortified Daniel, David, Joseph, Paul, etc., and who permits His servants to have vigor is capable of doing the same for you, too. I believe you have to trust Him! Jesus is indeed trustworthy. His mighty power is evident wherever we go, and men are helpless against such power that formed the mountains. King David describes the strength of God in the Book of Psalms: "*Before the mountains were brought forth, or ever thou hadst formed the earth and the world, even from everlasting to everlasting, thou art God*"(Psalms 90:2). In his letter to the Corinthians, the apostle Paul exhorts them to trust the Lord, the only viable source of power: "*Finally, my brethren, be strong in the Lord, and in the power of his might*" (Ephesians 6:10). Strength is the life and the light of God.

At night, Jesus will refresh you and in the morning He will strengthen you. And His force is compassion, divine mercy, joy and peace. Suffice it to say that we benefit with a stream of benedictions daily from Him. Thus, I realize how awesome is my King, and I believe He deserves our glory and our honor for all the beautiful things He has done for us. All in heaven worship and adore Him. What about you, my dear friend? Don't you need a Savior in times like these? I am pretty sure you need someone to grip and hold onto. You need a solid rock to grip firmly, and this is Jesus of Nazareth, the Rock of Ages. My friend, for too long you have purposely kept your eyes below instead of above. Isn't it yet time to look up above to Jesus and to discover His power? In your sickness and your disappointments, it is Jesus who gives you strength to continue your daily affairs, along with the sun, oxygen, rain and other essential elements that help ensure your survival. Very often, you feel weak and express dissatisfaction, and yet Jesus is very close. Wonderfully, there is so much around that stirs us to say loudly that the powerful force of God leads and supports the universe and His supreme promise of the return of Jesus. Just give Him thanks. Finally, the force of God is a power. It is the power of God that raised Jesus from the dead, because it is from Him that life comes. And the same powerful force will raise all the dead in Christ toward God. Feeling weak and discouraged? May be you are an innocent victim in prison? Remember the story of Joseph in Egypt. Then Potiphar, *"Joseph's master, took him, and put him into the prison, a place where the king's prisoners were bound"* (Genesis 39:20-23). But *"The king sent and loosed him; even the ruler of the people, and let him go free"* (Psalms 105:20). Find yourself in dire straits? Never doubt, my friend, Doctor Jesus will get you through these and other difficult circumstances. May the Lord strengthen you today and tomorrow! That is why the Gospel is a divine power that saves and redeems. Thus, you will live with Jesus everlastingly if you stay close to Him, since His power lasts forever and ever! Jesus loves you, and He is always there to sustain your faith, to deliver you, and to give you strength in your weakness! In fact, Jesus gives us strength to work and to mind our daily activities because only in Him do we find strength. You can be brave and strong because Jesus is with you and His power will free you and gives you strength!

A prayer:

Dear Father, please accompany me in my trip through life and place your force against my weakness. May I find support, sufficient courage to endure strain, and to have peace in Jesus! Amen.

My friend, your prayer will be answered in God's way and on His time. Be faithful and trust the Great Healer. His grace is sufficient in this world, and in the world to come! Unquestionably, Jesus offers and gives security and strength!

Chapter Six

Temptation and Help

Temptation is a desire for forbidden things. "The desire to have or do something that you know you should avoid."[12] It is an interior drive that attracts us to things that should be avoided. Assistance is needed to avoid these dangerous situations. Help comes from a superior power. "Temptation is a suggested short-cut to the realization of the highest at which I aim—not at what I understand as evil, but towards what I understand as good..." Oswald Chambers.

Temptation is a strategy conceived by Satan, our enemy, to make sin look like an attractive and beneficial thing to those who have a passion for the forbidden. Man is always confronted with a variety of tempt-ations, internal and external. Adam and Eve were tempted by Satan and gave in. We are also tempted every day, and our destiny is like that of our first parents. Satan seeks constantly to defeat us, and we are powerless before the danger of temptation. In fact, even Jesus was not exempt from temptation throughout His ministry of love. But He did resist temptation whereas Adam and Eve failed. André Georges put it this way: " Psalms 144:1, 2 proclaims that throughout the adverse circumstances of his life, David experienced God's mercy and His

---

[12] WordNet® 2.1, 2005 Princeton University.

goodness: '*Blessed be the Lord my strength, which teacheth my hands to war, and my fingers to fight...and he in whom I trust; who subdueth my people under me.*' But when he followed his own impulses, he had to take refuge in Gath, home of Akish. There as he walked in the balcony of his house, temptation came in the form of the adulterous look of Bethsheba (1 Samuel 27:1, 2; 2 Samuel 1). But as long as he walked with God he had no fear from his enemies."

Temptation is a tyrant that does not easily let go. Rich or poor, black or white, pagan or Christian, strong or weak: no one is exempt. When facing this danger, where do we find the force to resist? Does temptation come from God? No, it does not come from God! As the apostle James explained: "*Let no man say when he is tempted, I am tempted of God: for God cannot be tempted with evil, neither tempteth he any man: But every man is tempted, when he is drawn away of his own lust, and enticed*" (James 1:13, 14). As I said, Jesus knew temptation, and He needed God's power to resist all desire. That is why Jesus prayed frequently, so that He gained the power to confront the enemy. It is the same for you and for me. When we are facing temptation, we need to seek God's assistance through prayer and meditation. Eve is tempted in the garden and seduced by Satan. The Bible describes the temptation of Adam and Eve: "*And when the woman saw that the tree was good for food, and that it was pleasant to the eyes, and a tree to be desired to make one wise, she took of the fruit thereof, and did eat, and gave also unto her husband with her; and he did eat*" (Genesis 3:6). Jesus will give you the force to resist temptation and immoderate passion if you do His will. Always be faithful and true to Him. If you trust Him, there is an angel that guides your path day and night. And when the enemy comes, the Holy Spirit will chase him away. With prayer, the enemy must leave you alone and go away!

Joseph resisted temptation when Potiphar's wife tried to seduce him: "*And she caught him by his garment, saying, Lie with me: and he left his garment in her hand, and fled, and got him out*" (Genesis 39:12). Joseph fled from temptation leaving his clothes behind. God can help you resist temptations if you are willing to run from evil as Joseph did. Thus spoke the Lord: "*Because thou hast kept the word of my patience, I also will keep thee from the hour of temptation, which shall come upon all the world, to try them that dwell upon the earth*" (Revelation 3:10). My friend, if your faithfulness in God's promise is consistent, He won't fail you. If He is first in your life, everything else will fall into place. Your children, your spouse, your parent, your colleague, your friend, your neighbor may disappoint you, but not your Lord. He helped Joseph. He helped others. He helps me. He will help you, too in your temptation.

Jesus is tempted in the wilderness and chases Satan away. Doctor Luke expounds the temptation of Jesus. After forty days fastening in the wilderness, Jesus was very hungry: "*And the devil said unto him, If thou be the Son of God, command this stone that it be made bread. And Jesus answered him, saying, It is written, That man shall not live by bread alone, but by every word of God. And Jesus answering said unto him, It is said, Thou shalt not tempt the Lord thy God. And when the devil had ended all the temptation, he departed from him for a season*" (Luke 4:3, 4, 12, 13). What a victory for Jesus! And Satan, the tempter was chased away. The danger of temptation can take the form of pleasure, desire, false promises of wealth, enticing mirages and opportunities. These are Satan's favorite tactics, from the early times of our first parents, until today. Jesus Himself was tempted by Satan. However, Jesus won because He cried and called on His Father. So it is the same for us, because His Father is also ours and He is always ready to help us. Are you tempted? Jesus can help by giving you the power needed to fight temptation: Put all your trust in Jesus of Nazareth. Do not give way to the enemy's charming voice. Hide in Jesus, the Great Winner. If your life is threatened, I encourage you to go to Jesus because His Father is alive; He is of great help for people like you and me. In fact, you can always count on Jesus. In his writings to the Corinthians, apostle Paul says: "*There hath no temptation taken you but such as is common to man: but God is faithful, who will not suffer you to be tempted above that ye are able; but will with the temptation also make a way to escape, that ye may be able to bear it.* (1 Corinthians 10:13). Throughout life, we will always have to confront internal and external temptation. Since Jesus suffered temptation, He offers the promise of help to those who are tempted, that is why the prophet Isaiah says: "*For I the Lord thy God will hold thy right hand, saying unto thee, Fear not; I will help thee*" (Isaiah 41:13).

Do you believe that He can give you the strength to defeat temptation? Yes, to conquer temptation we need to resist with the grace of God. Obedience to His word is a powerful weapon against temptation. Certainly, if you do His will, you can surely count on Jesus' help and assistance. Fight, pray, and suffer temptation for Christ, and you will be victorious, as He promises. Resist internal and the external temptation knowing that suffering is inevitable, but God will give you the strength to defeat the enemy. Surely you will prevail if that is your desire. The word of God is the only resource for those who are tempted. Remember how Jesus prayed: *"And lead us not into temptation, but deliver us from evil"* (Matthew 6:13).

A prayer:

Dear Father, give me the force and courage to resist all temptation. Please, Lord, come to my rescue! I pray in the name of Jesus! Amen

If you ask God for strength to resist temptation, certainly He will do so. With Jesus it is His power, force and supremacy that protects us against all temptation. In the danger of temptations, look to Jesus. He is your refuge and your fortress. His grace is sufficient now and forever.

Jesus of Nazareth gives strength to weak, tempted and discouraged souls!

Are you tempted?

Jesus can help by giving you the

power needed to fight temptation.

"No temptation has seized you except what is

common to man. And God is faithful;

He will not let you be tempted beyond

what you can bear. But when you are tempted,

He will also provide a way out

so that you can stand up under it"

(1 Corinthians 10:13).

Chapter Seven

Selfishness and Jealousy

𝕴n the beginning…selfishness and jealousy "*and the loftiness of man shall be bowed down, and the haughtiness of men shall be made low: and the Lord alone shall be exalted in that day*" (Isaiah 2.17). Selfishness is the feeling of excessive self-esteem. "Characterized by or manifesting concern or care only for oneself."[13] It makes you believe you are above others. In fact, selfishness is presumption, deception, arrogance and revolt. Selfishness is a negative feeling that prevents the truth from coming out. The parable of the Pharisee and the Publican illustrates selfishness and humility in Luke 18:9. Jealousy: "resentment against a rival, a person enjoying success or advantage, etc."[14] Jealousy is the excessive desire to surpass others, and to prevent them from being happy, as if happiness exists just for oneself. Jealousy depreciates others, seeks to control and even harm them. At the same time, jealousy can be a positive force—a stimulus to improve oneself.

Me…myself…and I…

---

[13] Unabridged Dictionary, Random House, New York, 2006.

[14] Ibid

"I will ascend above the heights of the clouds;"

"I will be like the most High." Those are the words of king Babylon, a figure of Lucifer. What impertinence! Odious lies, excessive presumption of someone who wants to be the Creator and who believes he is very powerful (Isaiah 14:14). Obsessed by power, Lucifer seeks to supplant God. He was successful in convincing many angels of his cause, and that underlines the necessity of putting our trust in Jesus. Clearly, as the Bible expressed it: *"How art thou fallen from heaven, O Lucifer, son of the morning! How art thou cut down to the ground, which didst weaken the nations!"* (Isaiah 14:12).

Lucifer became Satan, the Deceiver. The Book of Ezechiel presents Lucifer as an Archangel who had it all: " *...Thus saith the Lord God; Thou sealest up the sum, full of wisdom, and perfect in beauty. Thou hast been in Eden the garden of God; every precious stone was thy covering, the sardius, topaz, and the diamond, the beryl, the onyx, and the jasper, the sapphire, the emerald, and the carbuncle, and gold: the workmanship of thy tabrets and of thy pipes was prepared in thee in the day that thou wast created..."* (Ezechiel 28:12, 13). For his rebellion, jealousy, and self-exaltation, Lucifer was expulsed from God's Habitation and is confined to planet earth. Today, the world is filled with anger, injustice, violence, immorality, senseless crime, and hate and we are suffering bitterly. That is why God says: *"My people are destroyed for lack of knowledge"* (Hosea 4:6).

The Bible states, Satan is preparing to launch his last powerful combat to prevent the return of Jesus Christ. It all began in heaven through the selfishness and jealousy of Lucifer. From a lack of loyalty, Lucifer lost heaven and convinced other angels to follow his rebellion. Thus began the hostility of the dragon, selfishness, a great danger. "Lucifer allowed his jealousy of Christ to prevail." And since then, the evil continues, causing tears, pain, suffering and death. Lucifer perverted the freedom God granted to His creatures. Men, too, wanted to be God, because our first parents rebelled against Him in manifest disobedience. The consequence of this disobedience is evident everywhere. But in Jesus we find the perfect antidote in His humility, which comes from truth. The Bible teaches us that God's jealousy and

Satan's jealousy confront each other: "*I the Lord thy God am a jealous God*" (Exodus 20:5). And Lucifer is a jealous angel. Is God's jealousy the same as Satan's jealousy? I would say no because God's jealousy is very constructive and Satan's jealousy is destructive. Lucifer became jealous of his Creator, his Benefactor, showing us how jealousy and envy possessed his heart.

Cain did not heed God's warning. The author of the Book of Genesis recognized the existence of Cain's jealousy. Cain made an offering of fruit to God; and Abel made an offering of sheep. God's eyes were favorable on Abel and his offering. Cain wasn't happy at all. And God asked him: "*Why art thou wroth? And why is thy countenance fallen? If thou doest well, shalt thou not be accepted? And if thou doest not well, sin lieth at the door...And unto thee shall be his desire, and thou shalt rule over him.* Cain *rose up against Abel his brother, and slew him*" (Genesis 4:6-8). Jealousy and selfishness stirred up Cain to kill. From then on, he knew no rest because he was always on the run. It is sad, indeed, and one may ask why did God disregard Cain's offering? Simply put, he failed to do what God asked him to do. (See Genesis 8:20; Leviticus 1.) If you are jealous of somebody's success and you feel unhappy or have an intense desire to capture another's honor or prosperity for yourself, it is time to tell Jesus all your fear, disappointments and hatred. And He will deliver you. Do not be jealous of someone's achievements because Jesus can do even more for you. Go, hurry up! Jesus is waiting for you and wants to help you! Unfortunately, many men and women rejected Jesus because they were selfish and presumptuous. It is written: "*And the light shineth in darkness; and the darkness comprehended it not*" (John 1:5). Men rejected Jesus' messages because they could not stand the truth. That is exactly what Satan has done in heaven, and today again his agents are doing just that on earth. Lucifer wanted to be on God's throne, and he became jealous of His Creator. He wanted to supplant God because he was full of knowledge, power, and unsurpassed beauty. Lucifer is a creation, but the object of his desire was God's throne, and he wanted to take the Almighty's power by force. I wonder if this dreadful attempt against his Creator was the original *coup d'État.*[15]

---

[15] (Politics), a sudden and violent change in government. American Heritage Dictionary.

God resists the proud and gives grace to the humble, says apostle James. My friend, selfishness and jealousy kill. That is why the apostle Peter expressed it this way: "For *God resisteth the proud, and giveth grace to the humble. Humble yourselves therefore under the mighty hand of God, that he may exalt you in due time*" (1 Peter 5:5, 6). Far away from selfishness and jealousy, you will walk towards heaven, your God's house, eternal sojourn, city of light, and you will be in the presence of Jesus, the Creator, forever and ever. Selfishness and jealousy are the twins responsible for our miserable condition. It all happened because Satan and the angels were given free choice. Adam and Eve, too, were given free choice. They failed the test. "And, we too have free choice. Yet, our situation is much worse than Adam and Eve's before the fall. The fall is a powerful example of what happens when beings with free choice make the poor choices," writes Dr. A. V. Wallenkampf. Selfishness and jealousy corrupt all and lead us to death, but God's grace gives life. Unfortunately, a great number of people refuse to accept God's powerful grace. Do not be too proud of yourself, as was Job, who believed he was just. In fact, God shows us that opinions lead to selfishness, pride, and vanity. Adam and Eve made the wrong choice. We, too, followed their path when most of us voluntarily rejected God's grace. Make no mistake, only the Holy Spirit and obedience can help us make the right choices.

Jesus loves us very much despite our sinful nature. His desire is to make us humble and sweet. My friend, surrender today to Jesus, and you will be healed. If you humble yourself, God will lift you up. God can do it and His support can put you in a position you can only imagine. He will do the same for you. Give Him praise in bad as well as good times. Jesus heals many people and He will do the same for you. Learn from Jesus because He is sweet and humble! Remember, selfishness as well as jealousy brings contention, deceit, intrigue, lies, and bitter fruit which divide and kill. Satan is the Great Deceiver. According to the Bible, Lucifer deceived some angels as well as Adam and Eve: "*The serpent was more subtle than any beast of the field which the Lord God had made. And he said unto the woman, Yea, hath God said, Ye shall not eat of every tree of the garden? And the woman said unto the serpent, We may eat of the fruit of the trees of the garden: But of the fruit of the tree which is in the midst of the garden, God hath said, Ye shall not eat of it, neither shall ye touch it, lest ye die. And the serpent said unto the woman, Ye shall not surely die"* (Genesis 3:1-5).

Today again, his agents keep doing the same on earth. The Great Deception is here and it will involve the whole world. Knowing that Satan is very clever, Jesus warned the disciples and said unto them: *"Take heed that no man deceive you. For many shall come in my name, saying, I am Christ; and shall deceive many"* (Matthew 24:4, 5). Beware the Great Deceiver. In any case, our merciful God will intervene to reclaim His creation. The apostle John reveals in Revelation chapters 12 and 20, the end of the ultimate battle: *"And the great dragon was cast out, that old serpent, called the Devil, and Satan, which deceiveth the whole world.... And the devil that deceived them was cast into the lake of fire and brimstone, where the beast and the false prophet are, and shall be tormented day and night for ever and ever."* Thankfully, we have Jesus, the Victorious, the Savior, the Deliverer, and His grace is sufficient. He is our Friend. What a wonderful Friend we have in *Jesus, the Great Healer*!

In the beginning everything was good: *"...and God saw that it (the creation) was good."* But selfishness, jealousy, and rebellion dig a deep hole in our life, pull us away from God and make us suffer bitterly. What we need today is humility, modesty, the spirit of forgiveness, love, peace, and unity in Jesus, our Redeemer and Benefactor. Yes, my friend, in spite of our revolt, God always intervenes in our distress with mercy, kindness, and compassion to heal and sustain us! (Genesis 1:21). Are you jealous of your friend's success? Are you envious of your neighbor's possessions?

A prayer:

Have mercy upon me, O Lord! I pray that you prevent me from nourishing the feelings of selfishness and jealousy. I recognize that I am a fallen being with a corrupted and sinful nature. Please help me to live in the light of your glory every day! Amen.

With Jesus it is humility, simplicity, wisdom and victory today and forever, since His grace is sufficient. Jesus heals selfishness, vengeance, jealousy, and presumption. The power of His blood will free you from selfishness, and jealousy!

Chapter Eight

Hatred

𝕎hat is hatred? "Intense animosity, hostility or dislike of just one or all living beings and sometimes of things."[16] Hatred is dangerous, sinful, and threatens our eternal life. It is inappropriate and inhuman to hate anyone. We must acknowledge that hate hurts everyone. Hate and racism are wrong. They are wrong against the teachings and practice of *Jesus, the Great Healer*. We are not powerless in the face of hate: we do our best and take positive steps to combat hatred. Sincerely, obedience and the Holy Spirit of God can help us achieve our goals.

As Joseph F. Delany writes in *New Advent*, a Catholic encyclopedia, "Hatred in general is a vehement aversion entertained by one person for another, or for something more or less identified with that other. Theologians commonly mention two distinct species of this passion: One (*odium abominationis*, or loathing) is that in which the intense dislike is concentrated primarily on the qualities or attributes of a person, and only secondarily, and as it were derivatively, upon the person himself. The second sort (*odium inimicitiae*, or hostility) aims directly at the person, indulges a propensity to see what is evil and unlovable in him, feels a fierce satisfaction at anything tending to his

---

[16]American Heritage Dictionary, New college edition, Boston, Houghton, 2000.

discredit, and is keenly desirous that his lot may be an unmixedly hard one, either in general or in this or that specified way."[17]

Since Cain's time, hatred has been with us. And there has been a world of hatred and suffering, even though Jesus came into our world to tear down its walls and roadblocks. Today again, we are facing so much hatred, misunderstanding, and reluctance to forgive. We need to put hatred away with God's grace and go on with our lives. Jesus came to remove the hostility that separates God and us (Isaiah 59). But the roadblock of hatred among society remains high. Hatred among neighbors, friends, brothers, sisters, parents, children, even among churchgoers grows like a cancer that is destroying our body. In his book, *The 7 Habits of Highly Effective People*, Stephen R. Covey says: "Many 'older' children go through life either secretly or openly hating their parents. They blame them for past abuses, neglect, or favoritism and they center their adult life on that hatred, living out the reactive, justifying script that accompanies it."[18]

Hatred is a sin that goes against our relationship with Jesus and with others. If we love Him we must avoid sinful things like hatred. There can be no room in your heart for hatred. When someone hates you, you must continue to love back, unconditionally. Why is there so much hatred in our society? Why is there so much hatred in our families, at work and school? Why is there so much hatred, even in the church of Jesus Christ? Man against man, nations against nations, husbands against wives, children against parents, brothers against sisters, so much hatred even among so-called Christians. Yes, Jesus' enemies wanted to destroy Him because they hated Him. They wanted to kill Him simply for speaking the truth. Often, your own family members, colleagues, friends, neighbors, classmates and roommates hate you for many reasons, and sometimes without cause. They want to destroy you because they do not want to hear the truth. They prefer, instead, to hear lies and only that. They want to destroy your reputation because of fear of rivalry, or a feeling of jealousy and envy. They are not comfortable with the truth. Enmity, antagonism, opposition, and a desire for

---

[17] www.newadvent.org
[18] COVEY, Stephen R. (1990). The 7 Habits of Highly Effective People, New York, Fireside, p.117.

vengeance can also grow into hatred. We need to embrace, reconcile rather than retreat. The time is now. We need love, tolerance, forgiveness and patience. Love, love…that is life. In fact, only God can take vengeance. That is why it is written: *"Vengeance is mine; I will repay, saith the Lord"*(Romans 12:19). Discrimination, insults, physical and verbal violence, racial slurs, lies, prejudice, abuse of power, and injustice provoke hatred. Isn't that why there is so much chaos on our planet? *"Be not overcome of evil, but overcome evil with good"*, said the apostle Paul (Romans 12:21). And he added: *"Now I pray to God that ye do no evil"* (2 Corinthians 13:7). Forgiveness and humility stop the spread of hatred. The time is now for love to overrule hate.

Forgive and love them in spite of all. In the Book of Luke, Jesus teaches us: *"But I say unto you… Love your enemies. …For if ye love them which love you, what thank have ye?"* (Luke 6:27-32). The Master teaches us to do our best to minister to or otherwise help them. We need to commit and to involve ourselves with them in a loving, caring, and respectful way. The difficult part, however, is to assist them in their deficiencies, since it is easier, much easier, to reject them and accept only those who are pleasant to us. We even feel justified in rejecting those who are unappealing to ourselves and to our cause. In his book, *Living God's Love*, Douglas Cooper writes: "But all the while we make it perfectly clear that we expect the unlovely to keep their distance and to know their place. Some we even feel justified in rejecting are: the hostile, the critical, those who seem always to cause tension and frustration. Those who make us feel uncomfortable and who seem forever spitting on other people with words. To us, these unappealing, unlovely souls we justify ourselves in rejecting."[19] But Jesus teaches us to love them all. Amos, the prophet of God, said: *"Hate the evil, and love the good"* (Amos 5:15). Hateful, ugly and hostile feelings invaded Esau because his brother Jacob lied and stole his blessings—proof that to lie is the worst perversion. In Genesis 27:1, 22, 23 we read: *"And it came to pass, that when Isaac was old, and his eyes were dim, so that he could not see, he called Esau his eldest son, and said unto him, My son: and he said unto him, Behold, here am I.…And Jacob went near unto Isaac his father; and he felt him, and*

[19] COOPER, Douglas. (1975). Living God's Love, Mountain view, Pacific Press publication, p. 42.

said, the voice is Jacob's voice, but the hands are the hands of Esau. And he discerned him not, because his hands were hairy, as his brother Esau's hands: so he blessed him." Jacob deceives Esau, and later on, his uncle deceived him. If you deceive others, others may deceive you down the road. Look how lies, dishonesty and shameless-ness are the products of active hate.

With a great sense of humor and simplicity, Jesus invites us to love one another. Jacob stole Esau's blessings, and the action caused a lot of anger and hate. Do not give the devil an opportunity to use anger to destroy unity and relationship with your sister and your brother. I urge you today to put away anger, vengeance, and hatred! Remember, hatred is dangerous. *"If we say that we have not sinned, we make him a liar, and his word is not in us"* (1 John 1:10). God expects us to defeat hatred and all animosity because they elicit quarrels. In talking with is Creator, David said: *"They compassed me also with words of hatred; and fought against me without a cause. For my love they are my adversaries: but I give myself unto prayer. And they have rewarded me evil for good, and hatred for my love"* (Psalms 109:3-5). In her poem, *Turn Your Eyes upon Jesus*, Helen Lemmel invites us to seek Jesus in times of trouble and dismay:

> "O soul, are you weary and troubled?
> No light in the darkness you see?
> There is light for a look at the Savior,
> And life more abundant and free!
> Turn your eyes upon Jesus,
> Look full in His wonderful face;
> And the things of earth will grow strangely dim
> In the light of His glory and grace. "[20]

In any case, *"Love and hatred are in God's hand,"* according to Ecclesiastes 9:1. God speaks through his prophet Jeremiah: *"The heart is deceitful above all things, and desperately wicked: who can know it?"* (Jeremiah 17:9). As for you and me, only the Holy Ghost can help

---

[20] LEMMEL, Helen. (1985). *SDA Hymnal* Number 290, Hagerstown, Review and Herald Publishing.

us control this negative feeling known as hatred. Always, we face two feelings: love that builds and hatred that destroys. They are very close to each other. Only God can control them. For Paul, the apostle of Jesus Christ, we must always put on God's love: "*And above all these things put on charity, which is the bond of perfectness*" (Colossians 3:14*).* We need to learn under the Holy Spirit's guidance to rise above hatred and angry feelings. Today we must seek out and love one another regardless of race, color and social conditions. The love of Christ must be visible through your actions toward a parent, a child, a wife, a husband, a brother, a friend, a neighbor, or a colleague. We have a common loving Father: we need to work, to play, and to live together in harmony, peace, unity and love in Christ. We need to build a loving relationship with humankind, for a better world for all. We need to repair broken relationships and forgive one another in the spirit of mutual respect and love. We need to believe in God and in His word—a belief that must be renewed every day. And we should stand for them regardless of the outcome. Yes! Love, love that is life! Wouldn't you like to taste the love and joy of Jesus? The most fruitful thing we can do in life is to share the joy of Jesus with others. Indeed, love, love that is life. God loved us first and unconditionally. Therefore, true love is unconditional, and if you need to find ways to maintain momentum in the fight against hate, go to Jesus today and you will be healed. Remember how Jesus stood one day in the midst of His disciples and said "*Peace be unto you*" (Luke 24:36). Jesus gives perfect peace, today, tomorrow, and thereafter. His blood whispers peace and rest forever and ever.

A prayer:

Have mercy, oh Lord! Take away anything that prevents me from loving sincerely. Please guide me from hatred to love, from war to peace, from separation to reconciliation. In Jesus' name, I pray! Amen.

Hatred is for the wicked. Jesus says, "*You have heard that it was said, Love your neighbor and hate your enemy. But I tell you: Love your enemies*" (Matthew 5:43, 44). Yes, my dear friend, you will be delivered from hatred, this chronic evil. Isn't it beautiful? Effectively, Jesus delivers from all evil. Wonderfully, Jesus' love conquers all hatred! I conclude this meditation on hatred with a thought from the apostle Paul: "*Let love be without dissimulation. Abhor that which is evil; cleave to that which is good*" (Romans 12:9).

May God pour His love and joy into you through His Holy Spirit! With Jesus, there is love, there is forgiveness, there is peace. He is a real and sure Counselor who consoles in troubled times, and always reveals Himself to us as a Brother. His grace is sufficient today and in the future. Jesus of Nazareth is love, and He is able to deliver us from all feelings of hatred and enmity. The power of His blood will free you from hatred!

Chapter Nine

Sickness

Sickness and Medicine

"Give doctors the honor they deserve, for the Lord gave them their work to do. Their skill came from the most High, and kings reward them for it. Their knowledge gives them a position of importance and powerful people hold them in high regard. The Lord created medicines from the earth, and a sensible person will not hesitate to use them. Didn't a tree once make bitter water fit to drink, so that the Lord's power might be known? He gave medical knowledge to human beings, so that we would praise Him for the miracles He performs. The druggist mixes these medicines, and the doctor uses them to cure diseases and ease pain. There is no end to the activities of the Lord, who gives health to the people of the world. My child when you get sick, pray to the Lord, and He will make you well. Confess all your sins and determine that in the future you will pursue a righteous life. Then call the doctor for the Lord created him and keep him at your side. There are times when you have to depend on his skill. The doctor's prayer is that the Lord will make him able to ease his patients' pain and make him well again. As for the person who sins against his Creator, he deserves to be sick."[21]

---

[21] *The Book of Sirach* 38, Today's English Version, p. 934.

The Doctor is in...

When you speak with your medical doctor,
you don't leave anything out, do you?
The same is true when you speak
with Doctor Jesus; do not leave
anything out. Tell Him your symptoms,
all your concerns. In fact, He knows them all, but He wants you to
nurture a father/child relationship with His Father. Isn't it sweet
and reassuring to have such a Brother? Also let Him know that you
are sorry for your sins.
"Don't cry, I am with you always," says Doctor Jesus.
The Great Healer has a clear picture of your condition, but He
wants you to talk to Him about everything that bothers you!
*"Indeed he was ill, and almost died. But God had mercy on him, and
not on him only but also on me, to spare me sorrow upon sorrow"*

(Philippians 2:27).

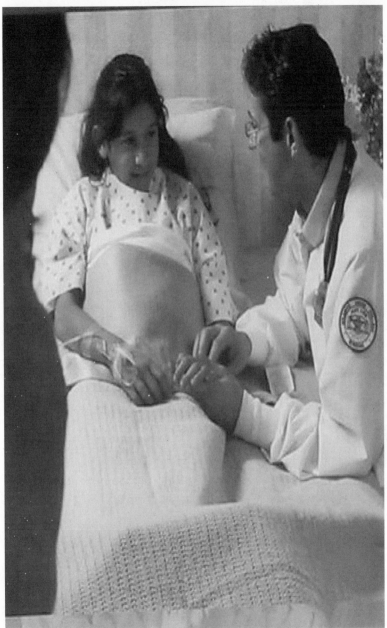

The suffering of men and women (Courtesy of AUC).

Indeed, Jesus gives life, eternal life.

He deserves

"the warm sunshine of praise"

for this great thing given—life.

What a gift from the Great Healer!

"For God so loved the world, that he

gave his only begotten Son,

that whosoever believeth in him

should not perish, but have everlasting life "

(John 3:16).

$\mathfrak{S}$ickness "prevents us from doing our physical duty due to impairment of part or all of ourselves, and makes us suffer," according to a medical dictionary. Even though many diseases can be cured or controlled by medication and modern equipment, they cannot prevent us from expiring sooner or later. How can we face the challenge of an acute illness? What can we do when feeling real pain? There are so many life-threatening diseases! One is more aggressive than the next. Very little is known about certain types of diseases that kill silently and quietly. But the Bible teaches us that disease comes from disobedience, sin, and rejection of God's law, and that it is sometimes used by God to discipline His children. In the face of all these diseases, where do we turn for healing and for refuge? We need someone to hold on to as an anchor in good as well as bad times. Only Doctor Jesus can immunize our system against all disease. Therefore, we need to turn to Him.

Job, extremely rich and God-fearing, lost all he owned and all his children. Satan was permitted to tempt him, and Job became covered with sores. He understood that God sometimes uses pain to chasten men. Still, Job cried out in anguish in his innocence and purity. He was mocked by his friends and even his own wife in his time of trial. He became sick and lonely with just a few so-called friends around to torment and reprove him with false accusations and other harsh words. Job cried out: *"As a servant earnestly desireth the shadow, and as a hireling looketh for the reward of his work: So am I made to possess months of vanity, and wearisome nights are appointed to me. When I lie down, I say, when shall I arise, and the night be gone? and I am full of tossings to and fro unto the dawning of the day. My flesh is clothed with worms and clods of dust; my skin is broken, and become loathsome. My bones are pierced in me in the night season: and my sinews take no rest"* (Job 7:2-5; 30:17). But Job remained patient despite all his adversities. In his suffering, Job prayed to his Faithful and True Witness, repented in the dust and ashes, asserted God's greatness, defended His justice and sought His wisdom and strength. And with the Lord's blessing, Job's fortunes were restored because he had faith in the living Redeemer. So should it be for you, too. Job, victim of unjust treatment from an enemy, remained faithful while his physical pain remained unrelieved. It is true that you are not Job, but the Great Healer stands nearby to soothe your pain. He will give you an injection to sustain your heart and to renew your health.

God is just, good and full of compassion. He is not the one to blame for our calamities and our suffering. We fail to comprehend that our disobedience of God's laws, as well as the negligence of some or all of the sanitary laws, is often the source of our disease. Are you ill, in pain? Jesus can help bring about your recovery as He did for the afflicted at Bethesda's pool. He did it for others. He can do it for you, too. Cry out your agony to the Man of sorrows, confess your sins and ask Jesus for forgiveness. Ask your enemies and friends for forgiveness, and forgive them, too. The healing process might take some time depending upon your relationship with Jesus or upon His will. His greater plan sometimes requires sickness, and we may never in this life fully understand His thoughts. Yes, men's knowledge is very limited. I invite you to meditate on God's word spoken through prophet Isaiah: *"For my thoughts are not your thoughts...,"* said the Lord. (Isaiah 8:9).

The prophet Jeremiah exposed the need of his people and cried out: *"Is there no balm in Gilead; is there no physician there? Why then is not the health of the daughter of my people recovered "* (Jeremiah 8:22). Isn't it sickness God's punishment? Sometimes, disease and tribulation can be a means of benediction and discipline in God's hands for His children. However, in sickness and persecution, God stands up for His servants. There is no disease that is incurable for Doctor Jesus. Trust Him. Go to Jesus and unload your burden on His shoulders, and wait patiently in prayer and meditation. Take God at His word. As Jesus healed Job and others, He will heal you, too. Do you believe it? You must, however, not dwell on what He is to do for you. Have patience and wait quietly for His deliverance. Praise His name every day and stay calm. Jesus has not forsaken you. Trust the Great Healer! Convinced of God's promise, David always finds grace, compassion and relief from his Lord, and he praises His name in Psalm 41: *"lessed is he that considereth the poor: the Lord will deliver him in time of trouble. The Lord will preserve him, and keep him alive; and he shall be blessed upon the earth: and thou wilt not deliver him unto the will of his enemies. The Lord will strengthen him upon the bed of languishing: thou wilt make all his bed in his sickness."* That is why we need to praise and glorify our Creator in all circumstances.

Often, our disease follows mistreatment of our own bodies from sleepless nights, tobacco, drugs, alcohol, bad diet and poor sanitation. In other words, intemperance may be one of the causes of our illness. In fact, "For every offense committed against the laws of health, the transgressor must pay the penalty in his own body." Sorely afflicted by illness, Job found peace and benediction only when He realized that he was nothing but a creature. This is a great lesson we need to learn from the patriarchal Job. If it is God's will for you to suffer more, let it be, and even if your physical pain goes unrelieved as you read this meditation, remain faithful as did Job, Daniel and others, because God is merciful and very compassionate. To everyone's surprise, one day I said: You will get up from this bed or stand up from that wheelchair without assistance because the Bishop of Souls is alive. Amazingly, He lives yesterday, today, and forever!

> "He lives, He lives, Christ Jesus
> lives today! He walks with me
> and talks with me along life's
> narrow way. He lives, He lives,
> He lives, salvation to impart.
> You ask me how He lives?
> He lives within my heart."[22]

Many have learned to know God in the midst of suffering! In times of illness and death men may come to realize how fragile life is. Go to Jesus in your miserable condition, and He will take care of your illness. Do not be like the "fools," David spoke of the: *"Fools because of their transgression, and because of their iniquities, are afflicted. Their soul*

---

[22]ACKLEY, Alfred H. (1985). *SDA Hymnal* Number 251, Hagerstown, Review and Herald Publishing.

abhorreth all manner of meat; and they draw near unto the gates of death. Then they cry unto the Lord in their trouble, and he saveth them out of their distresses. He sent his word, and healed them, and delivered them from their destructions. Oh, that men would praise the Lord for his goodness, and for his wonderful works to the children of men!" (Psalms 107: 17-21). In fact, the word of God heals and saves. Maybe you used to walk with God, and for some reason in the course of human events you stopped—and thus severed the relationship. That interruption may have lead into difficulties. You wonder whether this was the right thing to do. The only solution is to go back to Jesus and start anew, because He alone can give you hope, and life, again and again. Learn from your mistakes, and stay on the course Jesus has prescribed. Are you facing a sudden diagnosis and feeling afraid because your doctor has scheduled you for surgery? The Great Doctor will be in the operating room to perform the surgery skillfully.

Don't panic because the Great Healer is still in charge. If you want to resist the evil spirits, if your family's lives are on the line, if you are frightened, where do you turn for comfort? Seek Jesus' help today! Whatever your disease, whatever your sorrows, whatever your crisis, whatever your needs, Jesus has truly made provisions for you. All you need to do is speak to Him about your concerns. Even if the weather is ferocious, the storm more severe than ever, the tempests sweeping the surface of the deep ocean, with Jesus in your life the turbulence of the elements will come to an end. Are you exhausted, confused, scared, sad, and having nightmares because your mother has breast cancer, and you have been told you are at risk? Are you facing a frightening diagnosis and feeling afraid, upset, have no appetite, losing weight, having difficulty sleeping? Don't despair!

Someone is available to help. Do not fight alone. Go to Doctor Jesus and invite Him in, so He can help you fight the anxiety and even the disease itself. For He is: "... *mighty in battle*" (Psalms 24:8). Remember, these are battles you cannot win alone even if you are a good fighter; you must seek the Chief Cornerstone's help and counsel. Talk with Doctor Jesus. After all, you need your health and if you have got the Great Doctor, you have it all! Get up and go to Him. His office is open 24 hours a day, seven days a week. His consultation is free, and you can just walk in; no appointment required. Only *Jesus, the Great Healer*, can restore your damaged tissue and other cells and bring you back to health! My friend, in your sickness, Jesus is the only one who can get you out of your bed with a smile on your face. Just pray to Him, confess your sins and wait for His time. Remember, He is always on time. Only His plan will prevail. If you feel somber, your life is filled with disappointment and your soul is full with troubles, hang in there, and remember God loves you as if you were the only one on earth. Because He loves you He wants you to be healthy and happy. Clearer days are ahead and visible results are possible with Doctor Jesus. There comes a time when you have to let the Doctor look out for your health and your security, now and in the future.

Jesus fills the need of all thirsty souls. Perhaps you are very sick and you have physical or emotional pain, you are handicapped, frustrated and perplexed, your eyes fill up and overflow with tears. Is your doctor helpless, leaving you feeling lonely and wondering when you will get through this suffering? If so, go to "your Star of Hope" and to your Healer, who can restore your morale. He can help you carry your burden. He who can do all things said: "*Come unto me, all ye that labour and are heavy laden, and I will give you rest*" (Matthew 11:28). Stop crying! My friend, just go to your Advocate and tell Him everything. "*Casting all your care upon him; for he careth for you,*" said the apostle Peter. Wait calmly and patiently in prayer and give a chance to your body to catch up with your soul (1 Peter 5: 7). Christ has done a lot for you. Of course, He can heal you today! It is clear that your healing depends on you relationship with Jesus, but He answers your physical as well as your spiritual needs. He asks you to surrender to Him, and you will be healed and forgiven. Here is the catch, the secret of victory: every now and then, praise the Lord, celebrate His name and be grateful. Since He has brought you this far, He will not abandon you.

Regarding Lazarus' death, Jesus said: "*The sickness is not unto death, but for the glory of God, that the Son of God might be glorified thereby*" (John 10:14). He is your Father and your God. My Jesus is worthy of trust. No, don't let your faith fade away. The Great Healer is nearer than you think, and He is about to relieve your pain. You must not despair. Let not your courage forsake you. Voilà! Hence, the title of this book: *Jesus, the Great Healer.* Therefore, He can heal you today if you put all your trust in Him. Do you believe that? If you believe, you will see His power. Nothing is impossible for Him. You are not in this fight alone. The Chief Cornerstone is with you.

Jesus healed my mother. Some years ago, my mother suffered from a stroke. The prognosis was very gloomy. The doctors tried everything possible to save her, but there was little they could do. They admitted that they were helpless, and she went into a coma. Her doctor gave her three days to live; in fact, she remained in the coma for three months. I was trying to find answers by asking my God, "why my mother?" and "why this disease?" I thought about God's promises in times of trouble and distress, and I started to pray. Family and friends prayed, too, so that the Lord would let her be with us a little longer. Then she regained conscience. But she was not talking. We thanked God. He really answers prayers! According to His will, He answers prayer while we pray or even before we pray, as Prophet Isaiah states: "*And it shall come to pass, that before they call, I will answer; and while they are yet speaking, I will hear*" (Isaiah 65:24).

Thanks also to the diligence of my older brother and sister who kept faith and had tried everything possible to save Mom. Miraculously cured, God gave my mother the opportunity to talk again, which was a great victory for us all. She lived among us for a little more than three long, sweet years. This personally was a great blessing for me. I had the opportunity to visit my mother overseas well and alive for three good years before she passed away. For that miracle, I consider myself very blessed by God—in truth, it was an awesome experience with my Maker. Today, 21 years later, I am still very grateful to my Lord for that special treat. Jesus does what best for us. Perhaps you have a similar situation, and assume that the Lord has forsaken you. Be assured and trust God's supreme love! He is faithful and has not forgotten you. Whatever your mistakes and your shortcomings, stay faithful. Whatever the diverse circumstances of life you find yourself in today, and tomorrow, just ask Him to strengthen your faith. His promises will get you through. He can do the same for you, and even more. Only He can add more years to someone's life. You see, if you try to find answers away from the Bible, away from meditation, without doubt you will become discouraged. I urge you today to go to Jesus so that you can taste His love and His power! Our Heavenly Father promises to deliver those who love Him and obey His commandments: "*And the Lord will take away from thee all sickness, and will put none of the evil diseases of Egypt, which thou knowest, upon thee; but will lay them upon all them that hate thee*" (Deuteronomy 7:15). Truthfully, I am not only amazed by God's salvation plan but also by His divine approach—for mankind to stay healthy spiritually, mentally, and physically and live a vibrant, long, and disease-free life! Thankfully, our Jesus cares!

A prayer:

My Redeemer and my Savior, please keep me near the cross in my illness as well as in my health and have mercy upon me! Amen.

I invite you to follow the Lamb of God, your Redeemer and your Healer whether you are now in a hospital bed or at home in bed with pain. You may ask yourself when will your chronic pain go away? Trust the Lord. You will get up, today, tomorrow or in a month… regardless of the outcome. Cheer up, my friend, you will recover. Jesus will take care of you according to His promise! By the way, Jesus answers prayer. Be faithful and trust the Lord will do what best for you. Blessed is the man who trusts the Great Healer. With Jesus, suffering or illness don't really matter because He is the Doctor and His grace is sufficient today and tomorrow. Jesus of Nazareth gives complete health and delivers us from the fear of illness!

"Trust in the Lord with all thine heart;

and lean not unto thine own

understanding. In all thy ways

thine own eyes: fear the Lord,

and depart from evil"

(Proverbs 3:5-7).

Chapter Ten

Sadness

𝔖adness "is a simple emotion. When one is affected by unhappiness or grief; sorrowful or mournful. It is grief, with emotional or physical pain."[23] Affliction, exhaustion and depression take away joy and happiness. Sometimes we are sad from loneliness or from a lack of affection. The sudden loss of a parent, a spouse, a child, a friend, a colleague, a neighbor, or an animal brings sorrow and grief. And when one is unable to fulfill one's own needs, one is sad. The disobedience of Lucifer and men make God extremely sad. And God is still sad because men reject His grace and His salvation plan. Again today, men have forgotten Christ and are journeying far from Him and His word. The word of God is trampled, rejected, and forgotten. Men have forgotten the Creator and disdained all moral authority. Nevertheless, nothing diminishes the morality of God's word.

For our sake the Truth and the Life left heaven to come here for our salvation, and He encountered extreme suffering, sadness, and pain: *"Then saith he unto them, My soul is exceeding sorrowful, even unto death"* (Matthew 26:38). Finally, He was humiliated, beaten, tortured like a criminal and crucified. That is the suffering of our God. The Book of Samuel explains the sadness of David: *"When David was returned from the slaughter of the Philistine, the women came out of*

---

[23] Unabridged Dictionary, Random House, New York, 2006.

all cities of Israel, singing and dancing to meet king Saul with instruments of music. As they played, they answered one another and said: Saul hath slain his thousands, and David his ten thousands. Saul was wroth, and the saying displeased him. And Saul eyed David from that day and forward. After that, David departed from king Saul because he was afraid. The Lord was with David and Saul was yet the more afraid of David. David fled because Saul wanted to kill him." (See 1 Samuel 18.) In sadness, king David prayed to God. He cried out for God's help in Psalm 88: *"O Lord God of my salvation, I have cried day and night before thee: Let my prayer come before thee: incline thine ear unto my cry; For my soul is full of troubles: and my life draweth nigh unto the grave. I am counted with them that go down into the pit: I am as a man that hath no strength"*. If we have Jesus, even with sadness everything is well. In your heart you know God is good and has the final say. But are you desperate, overwhelmed with grief, stressed by the worries of life? This song, *I Must Tell Jesus*, invites you to tell all to Jesus, the Comforter:

"I must tell Jesus all my trials;
I cannot bear these burdens alone,
In my distress He kindly will help me,
He ever loves and cares for His own.
I must tell Jesus!" [24]

The Wonderful Counselor is always available to listen and help you carry your terrible burden. He's willing to talk to you at any time, day or night. You have access to Him seven days a week and twenty-four hours a day; just call Him in your prayer. Multiple occasions show that Jesus was available for everyone, day and night. Nicodemus, law doctor, one of the Jewish chiefs, went to Him very late at night and he was welcomed without complaint (John 3:2). Yes, you too, all of us are very welcome. He is our Brother, our Savior, and our Friend. In the morning, some came because of sickness, hunger, and demonic possession for healing; others came to trap Him or to stone Him. Jesus

---

[24] HOFFMAN, Elisha. (1985). *SDA Hymnal* Number 485, Hagerstown, Review and Herald Publishing.

was willing to answer their concerns, their questions, and their needs at any hour. At night, the disciples were tired and overwhelmed. They went to Jesus, and they were strengthened. He can do the same for you, too. He is always present every day, and He said: "*I am with you always, even unto the end of the world*" (Matthew 28:20). God is with you in your sadness. Reddened with anger and with a flood of tears, your feelings have been hurt or wounded. Your heart is saddened. Where to look for comfort? Go to Jesus. He is the one who is the source of joy. Willingly, God gives us everything, even His own Son. Surely, He can change our sadness to joy today and forever. So, no more tears, no more worries, no more sadness, no more death, no more sickness, no more pain, and you will know the beauty of eternity, the true joy. Yes, you will see the jubilation and happiness. That is why He invites us to be with Him forever and ever (Revelation 21).

However, to be with Him in His Kingdom, you must be humble as a child. On one occasion, when Jesus was asked by His disciples who would be greatest in the Kingdom of heaven, He placed a little child in their midst and said, "*I tell you the truth, unless you change and become like little children, you will never enter the Kingdom of heaven*" (Matthew 18:3). Very sad? All is lost in fire or flood? Very disappointed? Can't pay for your child's college tuition or your own? Divorce? Family problems? Can't live with him or her anymore? Life is too challenging? Working too hard? Burned out? Discontent and dismayed? Are you so disgusted, so saddened, so depressed, that you are thinking about suicide? The Wonderful Counselor can help you with your heavy burden. He will take away your sadness and give you joy if you decide today to live God's love and make every day of your life a blessing. In his Book, the apostle John quotes the word of Jesus: "*And ye now therefore have sorrow: but I will see you again, and your heart shall rejoice, and your joy no man taketh from you*" (John 16:22). The world is full of discouraged, confused, disturbed, defeated, angry, and sad people who need God's grace. Life is hell for a great many of them. Are you dejected, fearful, or weak? Are you a murderer, a drinker, a kidnapper, a drug addict? God still loves you, and wants you to join His Kingdom. The Man of Galilee can restore you, and He wants to save you. Remember, He died for you so you can enter His Kingdom. Jesus will give you joy, strength, rest and happiness according to His promise. As king David, wrote: *"Many are the afflictions of the righteous: but the Lord delivereth him out of them all"* (Psalms 34:19). Cast your sadness on Jesus. Only the Great Healer can put true joy in your heart, because He is the source of joy, life and happiness. Make Jesus your perfect Friend, and you will be joyful. The Bible teaches us that: *"Blessed are they that mourn: for they shall be comforted"* (Matthew 5:4). Look to your Savior who forgives you and changes your sadness to joy. Life with Jesus is joy, peace and security. Try Him, and you will see why those who have Christ in their lives always have confidence in God's promises because His "promises are forever." In fact, these are powerful promises for you to cope with life. The most needed power to cope with every situation. Remain faithful to Christ all the time until He returns! Voilà! I leave you with the Joy of the Wonderful Counselor! What a joy to trust and obey Jesus. It is a blessed assurance, indeed! His joy will take care of you.

A prayer:

My Lord Jesus! Please come to my aid! I am tired, weak, depressed, confused, and desperate. I have no joy, and every day I am sad. Have mercy upon me! Amen.

The Father, the Son, and the Holy Spirit understand your heart's desire and your sadness. only they can satisfy your needs today, tomorrow, and thereafter! Jesus promises to relieve all of your sadness and weeping to replace them with His joy and His happiness today and forever. With Him, you have been liberated, and your sadness has been transformed into joy. Gratefully, God's grace is sufficient today and tomorrow! Finally, with the Chief Cornerstone, you are "power up for life." Jesus of Nazareth gives vigor, energy, and joy in disarray and sadness!

Recognizing the distinctive Great Healer,

the Everlasting One, let us exalt Jesus of Nazareth

with His servant king David:

"Blessed be thou, Lord God of Israel

our Father, for ever and ever. Thine, O Lord,

is the Greatness, and the power, and the glory,

and the victory, and the majesty: for all that is in the

heaven and in the earth is thine; thine is the Kingdom,

O Lord, and thou art exalted as head above all.

Now therefore, our God, we thank thee, and praise

thy glorious name"

(1 Chronicles 29:10, 11-13).

"See now that I, even I, am he,

and there is no God with me:

I kill, and I make alive;

I wound, and I heal..."

(Deuteronomy 32:39).

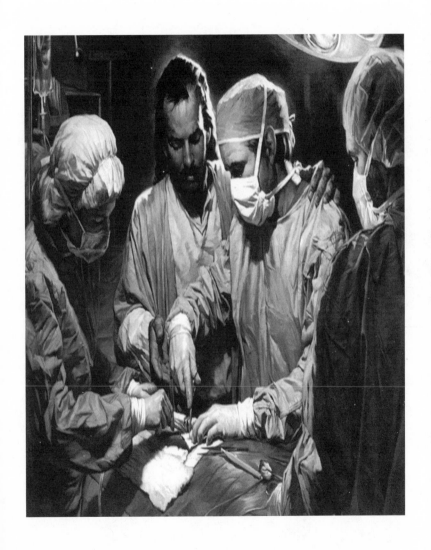

Surgical operation assisted by Dr. Jesus, Chief Surgeon (Courtesy of Biblical Perspectives).

In fact, there is no disease that is

incurable for Doctor Jesus.

He is a sympathetic Healer.

Trust Him.

Go to Jesus and unload your

burden on His shoulders,

and wait patiently in prayer

and meditation. Take God at His word.

As Jesus healed Job and others,

He will heal you, too. Do you believe it?

"And He touched the man's

ear and healed him"

(Luke 22:51).

Chapter Eleven

Healing

Healing is "the act or process of regaining health."[25] A medical dictionary defines it this way: "Healing 'in one sense' is the process required to get rid of disease—the series of progressive and interdependent steps it takes to restore health." Healing is also the deliverance from our sin. Healing can be physical, moral, and spiritual.

Missionary evangelist Sandy Sampson distinguishes five types of healing: "Divine, natural, medical, psychological, and demonic or occult healing. Divine healing is immediate, verifiable and permanent, *"And his fame went throughout all Syria: and they brought unto him all sick people that were taken with diverse diseases and torments, and those which were possessed with devils, and those which were lunatic, and those that had the palsy; and he healed them"* (Matthew 4:24). Natural healing may be given by the Creator to all living things. It may be slow and may not be permanent. Natural healing is sometimes difficult to verify. Although the glory belongs to God, man and modern medicine take all credit, he continues.

---

[25] Unabridged Dictionary, Random House, New York, 2006.

Sampson stated furthermore: "Medicinal healing may be slow or quick. Some medicines produce slow healing but with exceptions. A shot can instantaneously stop an acute pain, as can the application of ice to a burn. However, in both cases, complete healing takes time. The medical healing may be durable, but not always. Medicinal healing can also be verified easily. In general, all credit for medicinal healing has gone to men. Psychological healing is attributed to psychological factors. But God deserves all glory because He is the only Creator. Demonic or occult healing may be immediate or slow. It may be durable, but it is, in general, temporary and difficult to verify."[26] Above all, divine healing is, of course, the most trusted, the most glorious, the most blessed, and the most victorious of all healing that man has ever known. Spiritual, moral, mental and physical suffering is identified as the result of sin, from which Jesus powerfully redeems us.

King David healed by God. In his sickness, the psalmist admits that his soul was disturbed. He recognizes that only God can heal and deliver him: "*My soul is also sore vexed: but thou, O Lord, how long? Return, O Lord, deliver my soul: oh save me for thy mercies' sake. For in death there is no remembrance of thee: in the grave who shall give thee thanks? I am weary with my groaning; all the night makes I my bed to swim; I water my couch with my tears*" (Psalms 6:3-6). If God healed David His servant, He can do the same for you. Jesus is the Doctor, and He can heal you, too. Today is Tuesday. It is 11:30 P.M. sharp, and you are staring at the clock. It is virtually impossible for you to fall asleep. You are in pain. The doctor scheduled some medical tests on Wednesday morning, but the results were not as good as you had expected. On Wednesday evening, he broke this news to you: He needs to operate on you—tomorrow, at 7:00 A.M.—because the medication that was supposed to relieve your pain was just not working. You are scared, panicked, and afraid. Don't be too anxious about your worries and your concerns. On special occasions, Jesus, the Great Surgeon, comes by and takes control of everything. He takes charge of the case depending on the urgency of the situation. So you have the Best Doctor in house, don't panic. The following Tuesday after the surgery, the prognosis is still not good. The doctor has told

---

[26] www.yahoo.com/sandysampson

you he can't do anything more for you, and you have grown desperate. You feel shocked and helpless. Nothing seems to work, you feel torn, you are disappointed, and you are crying bitterly. Anything Jesus can do to help? Go to Him, pray, and wait for healing because His blood will heal you. Wait calmly, patiently in prayer and meditation, and you will see His power. Still, keep hope and faith alive. Jesus will take care of you, and you will be victorious. *Jesus, the Great Healer*, the Messiah, the true Shepherd brings the balm of healing and salvation. Yes, there is balm in Gilead! (Jeremiah 8). Remember King Hezekiah in his sickness. He prays and God hears the prayer and answers. The prophet Isaiah left the king's palace, but before he reached the street, God intervened and addressed him with His words, *"Turn again, and tell Hezekiah the captain of my people, Thus saith the Lord, the God of David thy father, I have heard thy prayer, I have seen thy tears: behold, I will heal thee: on the third day thou shalt group unto the house of the Lord. And I will add unto thy days fifteen years"* (2 Kings 20). And the king was healed of his sickness. Yes, there is healing in Jesus' blood. However, selfishness prevented king Hezekiah from glorifying God, His Healer, as he was should have. Always be grateful and thankful to the Master for His blessing.

Self-centeredness, pride, selfishness and covetousness: the attitude of King Hezekiah was an act of ungratefulness against God, who delivered him of his sickness. The king's action contradicted God's loving kindness. King Hezekiah failed to glorify and praise the great Father for His goodness and love in adding so many years to his life. For that unimaginable and unconditional love, we should be joyful in the Lord and give Him praise every day because He loves us so much. Besides, God is willing to love and accept you just as you are: rebellious, critical, disobedient, hateful and wicked. He wants to transform your life today if you so desire.

The Great Doctor healed by different means. And the people tried to touch Him because His strength healed everyone that was sick (Luke 6:*19*). In pain, Jesus gives comfort and heals by different means… through praying and fasting (James 5:14). Jesus heals through medical doctors (2 Kings 20:7). Jesus heals through miracles and the faith of the sick (Luke 5:12-13). Jesus' death brings us life, eternal life, if we accept Him as our personal Savior (Isaiah 53:5). Why doesn't God always heal us from our illness? Isn't it a way to make His love and His faithfulness available for all of us according to His promise? We often fail to comprehend why God would not sometimes heal even His faithful servant. Hopefully, you will know someday but it remains a fact, Jesus loves you. He is faithful and He wants you to be healthy and happy. Whether you are healed or not, remain faithful, and trust His will. Remember Jesus' prayer: "*Thy will be done on earth, as it is in heaven*" (Matthew 6:10). He knows what best for you. With a deepening sense of gratitude for His healing and deliverance, give praise and glory to the Great Healer. I encourage you to read aloud or silently some passages from the many beautiful verses in the Book of Psalms, expressive of joyful praise and thanksgiving (My suggestions are: Psalms, 138, 143, 146, 147 and 148).

Are you infected by disease? Feeling upset? Your doctor is helpless and the prognosis gloomy? There is only one physician available 24 hours a day, every day of the year, and you don't even have to leave your house to consult with Him or go to His clinic. That Doctor is *Jesus, the Great Healer*. It is indeed a blessed privilege to have free consultation through prayer. Meet Him today, because in Him you can find truth, grace, forgiveness and healing. With strong enthusiasm and love, Doctor Jesus heals the body, the soul, and the spirit. No, do not believe that the disease that wears away your strength is incurable. It is not so because Jesus healed yesterday, He heals today, and He will heal tomorrow. When your doctor admits that he's helpless about your pain and the complexity of your illness, and you are hopeless, don't despair. The Great Healer is in the house. You may ask yourself "Where is God?" when you are suffering. When will your disease find a cure? Bring your pain, your "why me?" or "why now?" and all your suffering to the Man of sorrows, and He will give you life again. Oh, my friend, my awesome Counselor is full of compassion and love. He is awesome in power, too! Praise the Lord and rejoice in His blessed promise. According to the Bible: you will be healed completely and live forever in a new place, free of disease, with your Maker. Wonderfully, the power of Doctor Jesus over disease is extraordinary.

We have a Great merciful Everlasting Father. Sometimes, we do not find the kind of healing that we are seeking; we grow sad and angry against the Lord. Still God is merciful and kind. Notwithstanding his long suffering and frustration, Job acknowledges faithfully and openly the greatness of the Alpha and Omega, when he says: *"Behold, God is great, and we know Him not, neither can the number of His years be searched out"* (Job 36:26). As I said earlier, someday we will know why on certain occasions He doesn't restore our body to health. Nonetheless, I invite you to meet Doctor Jesus because only in Him can you find peace and joy despite of your suffering. Wonderfully, only Doctor Jesus can brighten your spirit! With Jesus, all is well. He does all for our happiness. He is a balm to our injury, because He alone can calm and soothe our pain and heal us from our sickness.

Come, discouraged soul who suffers and cries, and the Lamb of God will comfort you, today, tomorrow and thereafter! Jesus offers love, hope, joy and security…today, tomorrow and beyond. He gives us so much joy, and He is willing to make us happy forever! Jesus of Nazareth, the Lion of the Tribe of Judah, the Great Healer, is the only answer to our illness because no one else have such healing power! "There is no one like Him."

-    Search… search as *"the deer panteth for the waters…"* and see for yourself if there is someone else like Jesus, the Bright Morning Star!

*"And the ransomed of the Lord
shall return, and come to Zion
with songs and everlasting joy
upon their heads: they shall
obtain joy and gladness, and
sorrow and sighing shall flee away"*
(Isaiah 35:10).

Chapter Twelve

The joy of healing

Rejoice

Be glad for the joy of healing,
Be glad for the joy of salvation;
A joy sent forth by God's blessing;
Be joyful on our voyage to Zion.

Look with confidence to our Maker,
The Great Healer of all Ages;
The Great Doctor, the Redeemer,
Jesus of Nazareth, the Rock of all Ages.

Praise the Father, the Son, the Holy Ghost,
From whom come the joy of eternity,
The days free of suffering, the heavenly host.
Yet in store comes soon the eternity.

With more joy than the days gone before and ever,
To be with Jesus of Nazareth, our Savior;
The road is bumpy, dark, long, and narrow, but not for ever.
Be glad, we will be soon with our divine Savior!

Doctor Jesus is a Great Friend who is always

there when you need someone to talk to today,

tomorrow, and every day thereafter.

What kind of friend is perfect for you?

Doctor Jesus is a total Friend.

He gives so much joy.

Oh! Amazingly,

His joy is sweet and full of grace!

" *Bless the Lord, O my soul, and forget not*

all his benefits: Who forgiveth all thine
iniquities; who healeth all thy diseases..."
(Psalms 103:2, 3).

A world of joy and happiness everlastingly (Courtesy of AUC).

"Courage, hope, faith, sympathy, love,

promote health, and prolong life.

A contented mine, a cheerful spirit,

is health to the body and strength to the soul."

Ellen G. White, Counsels on Health, p. 344.

Joy is something satisfying, valued and intimate. As one dictionary defines it: "The emotion of great delight or happiness caused by something exceptionally good; keen pleasure; elation. It is exciting, intense, ecstatic, and exultant." Joy is something we all need, so that sadness, suffering, pain and despair don't shatter our hearts and imprint on our memory deep and profound scars that make us bitter and angry, and destroy our dignity.

So many things give joy and make us happy. Some will say a word of encouragement or comfort, a simple laugh, a successful and secure job, the certitude of accomplishing an important task, a grateful act, sturdy health. Others will say a friendly and sincere handshake, the pride and joy of having a child, the joy of seeing a daughter or son's success, the joy of engagement, and the feeling of being appreciated by a colleague or a friend, etc. In a cold world, and heedful of sad circumstances, where do we find joy? Joy is a fruit of the Holy Ghost, as the apostle Paul tells us. And in Malachi 4:2 we read, *"But unto you that fear my name shall the Sun of righteousness arise with healing in his wings; and ye shall go forth, and grow up as calves of the stall."* In reality, Jesus promises and delivers us joy. If you look at difficulties, if you only pay attention to things that are not essential, a vain sadness will darken your face. Look instead to Him, and your face will shine with joy and happiness. Make the Man of Galilee your supreme Friend, and you will have happiness. Do not cry and don't loose faith, my friend, if you are afflicted by unhappiness and grief because the joy of Jesus will make you laugh and you will be joyful. When you are facing loss or blocked by difficulty, don't be discouraged by the problem's magnitude. Trust the Lord with all your concerns, since He will not abandon those who have confidence in Him. If you want to taste His joy, don't avoid His word, and don't overlook His will. His grace is marvelous and indeed exceeds your sadness.

Our Jesus never fails! In *The Physics of Star Trek*, Lawrence M. Krauss writes: "Newton's laws will continue to be as true a million years from now as they are today, no matter what we discover at the frontiers of science."[27] The same is true for our Maker. He remains the same God, and not even a bit of His character has ever changed. He will stay the same for a trillion years, or indefinitely, henceforth to eternity. Let me tell you, my friend, as an engineer I know that engineering systems, for example, always have a finite probability of failing. But my awesome Counselor, my Doctor, never fails. Try Him and confess your sins, forgive others, and He will give you a durable joy. To have the joy of Jesus, a peaceful rest and happiness forever, you need to understand that suffering is part of life, and that to suffer courageously without complaint is a blessed privilege. Also, you need to know that the joy of Jesus' presence can be disturbed by the enemy. That is why we need to pray constantly. In the midst of suffering, Jesus gives true and pure joy that can't be stolen. Come to the Faithful and True Witness and taste how sweet His joy is. I invite you to direct your eyes to the Advocate, because only in Him and under His marvelous grace can you find true joy that lasts. That is why His presence is needed everyday. For that I invite you to persevere in the joy of the second coming of Jesus. Undoubtedly, *Star of our Hope*, is around the corner, says William Knapp:

> "Star of our hope! He'll soon appear,
> The last loud trumpet speaks Him near;
> Hail Him all saints, from pole to pole.
> How welcome to the faithful soul!
> Descending with His azure throne,
> He claims the Kingdom for His own;
> The saints rejoice, they shout, they sing,
> And hail Him their triumphant King." [28]

---

[27] KRAUS, Lawrence M. (1995). The Physics of Star Trek, NewYork, Harper Collins Publishers, p.8.

[28] KNAPP, William.(1985). *SDA Hymnal* Number 174, Hagerstown, Review and Herald Publishing.

Listen! If you are overcome with sadness, if despair threatens you, if you are filled with disgust and sorrow, if your soul is exhausted, if after so many trials, so many persecutions, so much suffering and so much pain, your soul is sore, go to Him and seek His assistance. Sing a song to the Lord: "*Blessed assurance*" or "*Where you there when they crucified my Lord*", read a psalm of praise and victory, and give thanks because God is a loving Everlasting Father. Yes, *Jesus, the Great Healer* will provide for your needs as He promised. If you are in prison for whatever reason, today Jesus wants to be a real support for you. He is your Shepherd, your Redeemer, and a true Friend to lean on in times of trouble and distress. In effect, Jesus' beautiful and great promise is part of the grace only He offers. This joy that the word of God has spoken of is that which maintains, and lasts in spite of fear, worries, anguish, and even insecurity and other unpleasant circumstances. Jesus' joy is perfect. The birds seem, in effect, joyful and happy. You, too, will know this joy if you make Jesus your King. Psalms 34:5 expresses it clearly: "*They looked unto him, and were lightened: and their faces were not ashamed.*" God makes happy His children, the sick and others who suffer. Doesn't God do it for us even in the midst of suffering and pain?

God is a loving Father who wants to give us everything. Sometimes, you pray and you think that He doesn't respond to your request as you expected. And yet God hears, understands and answers accordingly, if only you put all your trust in Him and wait patiently. He never breaks His supreme promise. He is faithful. However, there is something that prevents us from tasting His joy, and that is our attitude toward His word. Your true joy must come from Jesus only. It can be yours. Are you ready to grasp today this beautiful promise of Jesus? Finally, don't you realize that *Jesus, the Great Healer*, is an extraordinary Man? Don't you need to have Jesus as your preferred Friend? Don't you want to taste the joy of Jesus? Oh! Yes, wonderfully, His joy is sweet and full of grace.

Heartaches, fears, tears, sorrows, worries, heavy labors, tribulations, persecutions, trials, and all "burdens are lifted at Calvary". Soon and very soon, our suffering will be over because of His supreme and precious sacrifice. My friend, Jesus is risen. Be happy and shout glory to the Great Healer for His wondrous love. Always stand on the promises of God. If our promises are frequently broken, it is very comforting to know that throughout the ages God always keeps His promises. "We will see Jesus someday." Parents, brothers, sisters, husbands, wives, children, friends, and all we have loved will be with Jesus. Look, Jesus is marvelous and stands ready to save you and your family. He is full of love and compassion, and His grace builds patience and endurance. Be grateful, joyful, and make a feast to the Great Healer! Our Jesus is the source of life and true happiness! The Chief Cornerstone may be yours, too!

Oh! My friend, my Jesus is indeed the only anchor that keeps your soul steadfast and joyful no matter what! Jesus gives us so much joy, and He will deliver us from misery and suffering, pain and all heavy labor forever and ever when He returns! Just obey His words, humble yourself, do His will, and let Him take over. With the Chief Cornerstone, it is peace and unspeakable joy that nothing can ravish, because Jesus gives life, happiness, joy and lasting peace. His grace is sufficient now and in the new life to come. Faithfully, the presence of Jesus of Nazareth brings healing and pure joy, perfect peace, true happiness, and deliverance!

" *Let not your heart be troubled: ye believe*

in God, believe also in me.

In my Father's house are many mansions:

if it were not so, I would have told you.

I go to prepare a place for you.

And if I go and prepare a place for you,

I will come again, and receive you unto myself;

that where I am, there ye may be also"

(John 14:1-3).

What a marvelous Man is Jesus.

He is all we will ever need!

Let us get ready for the

second coming of Jesus, our Lord of lords,

King of kings, the Great Healer!

Great is our Bright Morning Star, our Healer!

He is worthy of praise.

Trust Him, obey Him, and lift up your voice to sing His grace and His goodness. Give Him thanks because He is worthy of Glory. After all, Jesus of Nazareth delivers the care you need, when you need it. Whether you are ill, deaf, blind, paralyzed or otherwise afflicted, He provides as promised. In the near future, He promises a clean and perfect world free of suffering, hunger, discouragement, ungratefulness, temptation, selfishness, hatred, sickness, sadness, and pain. A world of joy and happiness forever and ever! Isn't it wonderful? My dear friend, do not now or ever settle for anything less than the very best, which is Doctor Jesus!

Conclusion

What have we learned?

To conclude these meditations, I tell you once again, Jesus loves and cares for you very much. Our Bishop of Souls showed the stars to the sinner and the lost. He gives back hope to the anguished and despairing man. He invigorates the tired and the discouraged man. He puts His hand on the foreheads of the sick, heals them, and gives them strength. He gives joy and peace to the persecuted. Isn't it reassuring to know we have a living God we can trust?

- He came to us knocking on our door, but we don't pay attention to His call. We have learned from this book to anchor onto Jesus when life gets tough. We need to love one another. It is best to have an "attitude of gratitude." This book teaches us how to live God's way. Ask Him for wisdom, and He will give it to you as He promised.

- Do you love the Man of sorrows? Wonderful! But do you live the way Jesus wants you to live? We need to learn to have confidence and the assurance that what we hope for is waiting for us. We know it's there, even though we cannot see it ahead. Do you have an excuse to continue avoiding God's word? I believe no, because you have so much to gain if you make Jesus, your Redeemer, your Great Role Model, and your Star of Hope. Where are you in your relationship with Jesus? Is He for you an ordinary or an extraordinary man, or even a Great Healer? Won't you finally walk with Him? Remember, it is the Chief Cornerstone who makes us strong and protects us from Satan.

- Jesus of Nazareth is all-powerful. He can do all for you. What else more can you ask? What are you waiting for? From Him alone come the healing and the deliverance. He stands ready to help in the diverse circumstances of life.

- Don't you need such a Savior? Remember, you cannot ignore Him and get away with it, and you have so much to lose if you keep ignoring the Maker. Finally, Jesus says: Look, I am here to heal and to bless you!

- Certainly, Jesus of Nazareth possesses the balm that heals! I hope you realize that without Jesus, life is meaningless. Thus, our God of deliverance can put an end to sin, and He promises the complete healing of our illnesses today, and tomorrow. Indeed, with the Bishop of Souls a better way of life is definitely waiting for you. The Almighty gives so many wonders and treasures, even His unique Son, to remind us of His love and His Kingdom. Aren't you thrilled by this Man of sorrows, the Great Healer, the Wonderful Counselor?

"And after these things I heard a great voice of much people in heaven, saying, Alleluia; Salvation, and glory, and honor, and power, unto the Lord our God"
(Revelation 19:1).

The greatest invitation

Have these meditations provided

you with some relief?

Have you ever been this refreshed?

If you are still thirsty, come, says

Jesus, the Great Healer:

"All you who are thirsty, come to the

waters; and you who have no money,

come, buy and eat!

Come, buy wine and milk without

money and without cost.

Incline your ear, and come

unto me; hear,

and your soul shall live; and I will

make an everlasting covenant with you"

(Isaiah 55:1-3).

Get help today with *Jesus, the Great Healer*.

Be safe always with the Chief Cornerstone.

Remain safe all the time with

The Lion of the Tribe of Judah.

Because we find the most comfort

and assurance only with the Holy Spirit.

What more comfort and assurance do we need?

The Maker gave it all, *Jesus, the Great Healer*,

the Savior, the Redeemer, the Best of an

awesome Everlasting Father!

In the end, I proudly recommend

Jesus, the Great Healer because with

Him peaceful and "happy moments roll."

Amazingly, "there is none like Him."

May the grace of *Jesus, the Great Healer*

help you keep your eyes on things above!

Jesus' second coming.

The biggest event of all time is around the corner.

Get ready for the most wonderful event of all!

"Every eye shall see Him" (Revelation 1:7).

About the author

Ernst Saint-Louis is an electronics engineer.
He holds professional certificates for additional training in information technology, electro-mechanical computer technology, religion, and a Federal Communications Commission (FCC) Radio broadcasting license-preparation program certificate.
Ernst is a Church Elder and is certain of two things: his calling to science and his calling to the ministry. As a man of faith he is fully committed to both.
He is passionate about God's plan for salvation and His divine purpose—for mankind to be healthy spiritually, mentally, physically and to live a fulfilling life.
He holds certificates in "*Jewish Biblical Doctrines*" from the
Israelite Heritage Institute, Newburgh Park, California,
and in "*Paulinian Studies*" from the
Salève Adventist University, CFME,
Collonges-sous-Salève, France.
Engineer Ernst Saint-Louis resides in Mahopac, New York.

Life is a journey.

Enjoy it with *Jesus, the Great Healer.*

Take His counsel to heart!

The Prince of Peace is a True Friend and a Wonderful Counselor.

Enjoy His Friendship and His Counsel!

The Lamb of God is the only Faithful and True Witness.
So may we be faithful and true!

" …all human wisdom was contained

in the two words. Wait and Hope!"

Alexandre Dumas

The Count of Monte Cristo

But Jesus, the Great Doctor

is all you will ever need

because He is still the answer!

After all, it's only natural to want

to share what you believe in!